Music Theory

A SYLLABUS FOR TEACHER AND STUDENT

VOLUME II

MUSIC THEORY

A SYLLABUS FOR TEACHER AND STUDENT

Ellis B. Kohs

School of Music, University of Southern California

VOLUME II

NEW YORK · OXFORD UNIVERSITY PRESS

1961

© 1961 by Oxford University Press, Inc.
Library of Congress Catalogue Card Number 61–5079

Sixth printing, 1977

Some of the material in this book was originally published in *Syllabus: Music Theory,* four volumes, copyright 1954, 1955, 1956 by Ellis B. Kohs

PRINTED IN THE UNITED STATES OF AMERICA

Preface

This work is designed for a three-semester or a two-year program of class instruction in theory, in colleges or conservatories. It is derived from the author's experience in teaching the subject, and explores some areas of thought that have been only suggested, or even omitted from, other works on harmony and music theory.

Particularly it seeks to increase an awareness of the relationship of harmony to form, and to assist in developing a more consistent system of harmonic figuring for diatonic harmony. Additionally it proposes a system for a realistic analysis of chromatic harmony, and examines turn-of-the-century developments, particularly the impressionistic style associated with Debussy and Ravel. It includes several short but complete compositions, as well as extended excerpts illustrating the growth of harmonic vocabulary from Corelli to Scriabin. There are a few short examples illustrating certain aspects of music from Gregorian chant to Hindemith. All unidentified items should be attributed to the author.

Supplementary reading and written assignments are provided. The suggested sight-singing, keyboard, and dictation exercises can assist in developing basic skills in vocal sight-reading, keyboard improvisation, and the capacity to translate into musical notation the sounds heard by the ear.

The author wishes to thank G. Schirmer & Co.; Associated Music Publishers; Boosey and Hawkes, Ltd.; Durand & Cie, Elkan-Vogel Co., American agents; and International Music Co., for permission to quote excerpts from works of which they hold the copyright.

To the members of the faculty of the School of Music of the University of Southern California who contributed helpful suggestions when the preliminary draft of this work was being prepared, and particularly to Mr. Leon Kirchner and Mrs. Jeanne Shapiro Bamberger, who contributed many stimulating thoughts, to Dr. Raymond Kendall for his support and encouragement, and to the many students whose penetrating questions and inquiring minds have helped the writer to clarify his own thoughts and reset his sights—to all these the author wishes to express his warm thanks.

E. B. K.

Los Angeles
November 1960

Suggested Supplementary Materials

The author has found the following supplementary materials very useful. Items marked by an asterisk (*) should be in the possession of each student. It is suggested that the others be made available for reference in the school library.

It should be noted that works recommended for examination are not necessarily endorsed in whole or in part by the author. Nor should it be assumed that works not cited here are lacking the author's endorsement. In some instances the student has been asked to consider points of view not wholly in agreement with those held by the writer. It is hoped that students will be encouraged to develop the capacity to judge and weigh, and to form habits of independent thinking.

TEXTS

William Mitchell, *Elementary Harmony,* Prentice-Hall, New York, 2d. ed., 1948.

Walter Piston, *Harmony,* W. W. Norton and Co., New York, 1941; rev. ed., 1948.

Roger Sessions, *Harmonic Practice,* Harcourt, Brace and Co., New York, 1951.

MUSIC

*Johann Sebastian Bach, *371 Harmonized Chorales,* (ed. Albert Riemenschneider), G. Schirmer, New York.
    (The figured chorales in this edition are of particular value for keyboard harmony.)

*Johannes Brahms, *Works for the Piano,* Vol. II.
    (There are several satisfactory editions. One might consider the edition of G. Schirmer or the convenient and inexpensive pocket-size edition (#66) issued by Lea Pocket Scores, New York.)

* Wolfgang Amadeus Mozart, *Sonatas and Fantasias for the Piano.*
    (There are several satisfactory editions. The two-volume set issued by Lea Pocket Scores is a convenient and inexpensive pocket-size edition.)

A sight-singing manual of the instructor's choice may be used to provide exercises in addition to those included in this work. The works of Bach, Brahms, and Mozart cited above may supply materials to be chosen at the discretion of the instructor.

Contents

Music Autographing by Maxwell Weaner

Music Theory

A SYLLABUS FOR TEACHER AND STUDENT

VOLUME II

I

Modulation (Part One)

The concept of modulation emerged rather slowly and intuitively in the course of musical history. It involves the notion that one tonic (or tonal center) may be abandoned in favor of another, perhaps only temporarily. Awareness of a tonal center is quite subjective, and the tonic quality itself may be elusive. It is therefore a more difficult subject to deal with technically than if it were an altogether objective phenomenon. In order to understand and write modulations, one might first consider the elements that provide or create a single tonal center.

The tonal center is not always immediately evident in a musical work. See the opening measures of Beethoven's Symphony no. 1, the beginning of the finale of his Piano Concerto no. 4, and the slow introduction to Mozart's C Major ("Dissonant") String Quartet. See also the controversial ending of Richard Strauss's tone poem, "Also Sprach Zarathustra," which alternates between two different tonal centers. To understand the nature of the problem, it is suggested you examine carefully and discuss in class Example I below. See also the opening phrases of selected examples in the Appendix.

The following factors are important in establishing the sense of key or tonal center:

    (1) the scale materials that are employed;
    (2) the function of chords and phrases in broad context;
    (3) the preparation and realization of a cadence.

Modulation involves the following elements:

    (1) establishment of an initial tonal center;
    (2) a point of transition or connection, frequently a single chord;
    (3) the establishment of the new tonal center, usually by a strong cadence.

The word "establishment" here is most important for several reasons. First of all, the sense of the old key must be removed by one means or another (usually a chromatic alteration). Secondly, there must be sufficient melodic and harmonic materials in the new key to make the change definite and unmistakable. What constitutes a sufficiency should become more clear as you have practice in analysis and writing. In general, you will find that all three of the primary harmonic functions (subdominant, dominant, and tonic) of the new key will be present, though this is not an absolute requirement. The new key is usually established or confirmed by a strong cadence (authentic or half).

The modulatory process is often a gradual one, as shown in this diagram:

Tonic	(Optional: chords removed from the tonic)	Chord common to both keys	Chord removed from the new tonic, e.g. II or IV	Cadence to V or to I in the new key
First key. . . . . .Second key				
—————————————————— (Pivot) ————————————————⟶				

The Common Chord. This chord acts as a pivot or connection between the two keys. It has the quality of a double meaning since it is analyzed one way in terms of the first key and another way in terms of the second key. This double meaning should always be shown in your analysis. Note that the symbols used under the bass line are on two different levels to make clear to the eye the shift of key at the point where the common chord occurs.*

The number of keys to which one can modulate by this means is considerable. Some of the possibilities have been indicated in Example II.

Example I. A Problem in the Establishment of Tonality (Tonal Center).

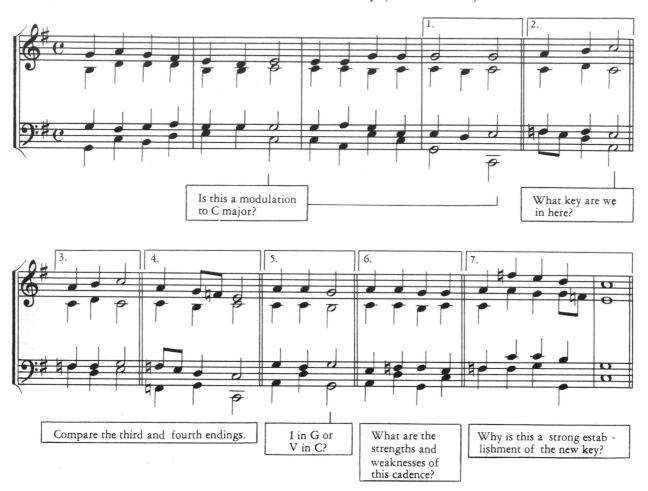

Example II. Modulatory Possibilities from C Major Using the C Major Triad as the Pivot.

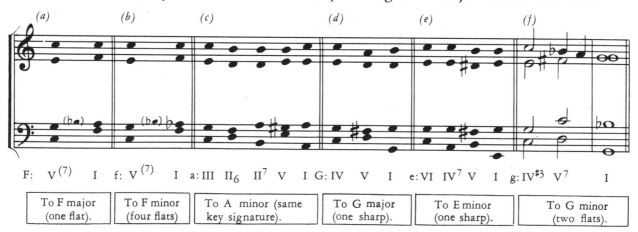

---

* See further: Walter Piston, *Harmony,* W. W. Norton and Co., New York, 1941; rev. ed., 1948; Ch. 8. See also Ex. (d) below.

SUGGESTED READING

Mitchell, *Elementary Harmony,* Ch. 18, pp. 211–20. Discuss his Example 401: is this really a modulation to a new key? Discuss also Examples 403a and b, comparing them with 401.

Sessions, *Harmonic Practice,* Ch. 9, pp. 267–72. Note also the exercises involving realization from figures, from basses, and from melodies in the latter part of the chapter.

Piston, Ch. 8. Note especially his Example 138 which shows the harmonic scheme (reduction), the harmonic rhythm, and the analysis of the common chord modulation. See Exercise 7 at the end of the chapter.

SUGGESTED EXERCISES

(a) Practice singing modulating melodies, using syllables or numbers. Look at each melody before singing it, decide where the modulation takes place (the pivot), and change to the new number or syllable at that point or on a tone immediately preceding it. For example:

(b) Use Bach chorales for further analysis, dictation, and keyboard harmony.

(c) Using Example II as a model, explore the possibilities of the II chord for modulation purposes; likewise the VI, III, and IV chords in the keys of D major, D minor, Eb major.

(d) Modulate to the suggested keys. Analyze, showing a : V as the pivot (common chord), and following the model provided.

II

Chromatic Nonharmonic Tones

We shall be concerned in this chapter not with chromatically altered chord tones, but rather with chromatically altered nonharmonic tones. It is suggested that the student review the material on diatonic (unaltered) nonharmonic tones in Chapters IX, X, XXII, and XXVIII of Volume I.

The Chromatic Neighboring Tone. The lower N.T. (or auxiliary) is sometimes raised or sharped. Thus 5-4-5 could be altered to 5-♯4-5; 3-2-3 could become 3-♯2-3, and so forth. Tones whose upper diatonic neighbor is a *half*-step away should not be raised (3 and 7 in major; 2, 5, and raised 7 in minor) unless the note of resolution has also been raised: thus, in C major you would use an E♯ only if it resolved to an F♯, which in turn would resolve to the diatonic 5th degree, G.

Example I. The Lower Neighboring Tone Chromatically Raised.

The upper N.T. is rather less commonly lowered or flatted. Although it is attracted (like the lower N.T.) more strongly to the note of resolution than the unaltered tone would be, the characteristic "leading tone" function from below is absent. One may occasionally find 5-♭6-5, 6-♭7-6, or 1-♭2-1, but the lowered upper N.T. is not used where the diatonic neighbor is a half-step away: thus you would not write 7-♭8-7, since these notes sound the same. This is a further application of the principle explained in paragraph one above.

Example II. The Upper Neighboring Tone Chromatically Lowered.

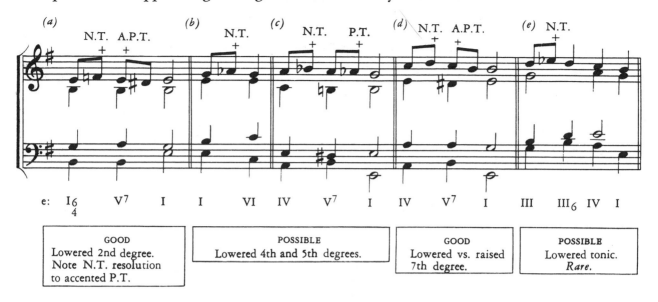

GOOD	POSSIBLE	GOOD	POSSIBLE
Lowered 2nd degree. Note N.T. resolution to accented P.T.	Lowered 4th and 5th degrees.	Lowered vs. raised 7th degree.	Lowered tonic. *Rare.*

The Chromatic Passing Tone. The P.T. may be employed in chromatic succession, either descending or ascending. One generally uses the raised forms when ascending, and the lowered forms when descending, except that ♯4 is more commonly used in a descending progression than ♭5.

Example III. The Chromatic Passing Tone.

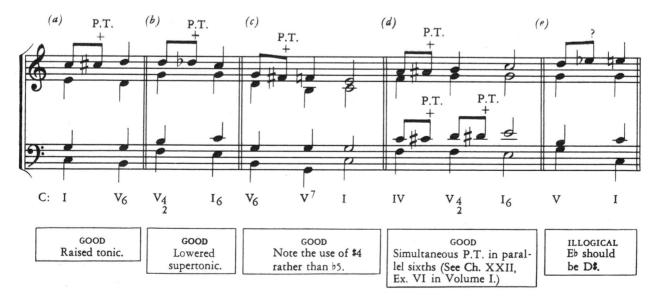

GOOD	GOOD	GOOD	GOOD	ILLOGICAL
Raised tonic.	Lowered supertonic.	Note the use of ♯4 rather than ♭5.	Simultaneous P.T. in parallel sixths (See Ch. XXII, Ex. VI in Volume I.)	E♭ should be D♯.

The Chromatic Changing Note Group. One or more tones in the group may be chromatically altered. One should observe care in seeing that the altered notes are spelled correctly in terms of their resolution to other chromatically altered tones or to diatonic (unaltered) tones in the key.

Example IV. The Chromatic Changing Note Group.

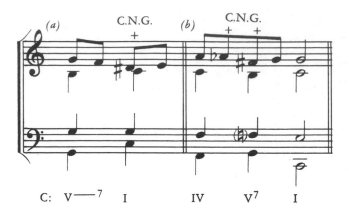

The Chromatic Double N.T. This four-note group is found occasionally in such form that the upper N.T. is lowered and the lower N.T. is raised. The note of resolution (the fourth tone) is, of course, doing double duty as resolution for both chromatic tones.

Example V. The Chromatic Double N.T.

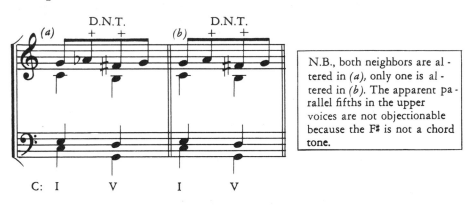

N.B., both neighbors are altered in *(a)*, only one is altered in *(b)*. The apparent parallel fifths in the upper voices are not objectionable because the F# is not a chord tone.

Other Chromatically Altered Nonharmonic Tones. In similar fashion it is possible to chromatically alter the échappée, the unprepared neighboring tone, and the appoggiatura. The decorated resolution of a suspension may include one or more altered tones.

Example VI. Other Chromatically Altered Nonharmonic Tones.

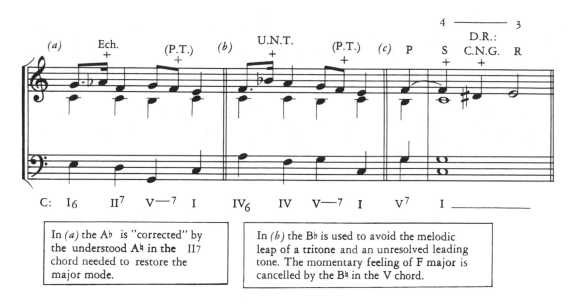

In (a) the A♭ is "corrected" by the understood A♮ in the II7 chord needed to restore the major mode.

In (b) the B♭ is used to avoid the melodic leap of a tritone and an unresolved leading tone. The momentary feeling of F major is cancelled by the B♮ in the V chord.

One useful general rule is that *chromatically altered tones resolve in the direction of alteration.* Like most rules this, too, has its exceptions, but they do not invalidate the principle. Keep in mind, also, that chromatically altered tones should be used in such a way as to be consistent with the logical and expressive demands of the melodic line, with the context, and with the harmonic style in which you are working.

SUGGESTED EXERCISES

(a) Reharmonize several Bach chorale phrases to illustrate usage of chromatic nonharmonic tones. Try to employ one or two of each type in each example.

(b) Supply harmonizations for each of the following melodic lines. Notes marked with a cross (+) should be treated as non-harmonic tones.

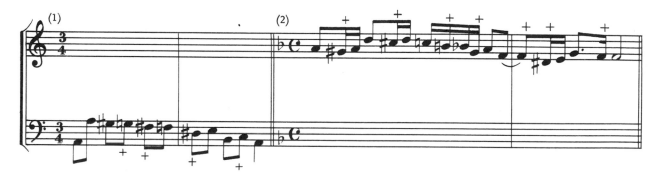

(c) Play the following progressions at the keyboard. Play again, embellishing each phrase with one or more types of chromatic nonharmonic tones.

I IV II V I
I III VI IV I
I IV I$_6^4$ V I

I II VI I$_6^4$ V I
I I$_6$ IV IV$_6$ I
I IV VII$_6$ III V$_6$ I

(d) Sing, using syllables or numbers. Identify probable nonharmonic tones.

(e) Write a melody with several chromatic alterations. It should be eight to twelve measures long and the phrases should be indicated by slurs, as in (d) above. Identify alterations according to type.

(f) Dictation of melodies and harmonic progressions illustrating chromatic nonharmonic tones.

III

Chromatically Altered Chords (Part One)

An altered chord is one that contains one or more tones foreign to the key. There are many different forms and types of altered chords, but the one most commonly encountered in the music of the classical and romantic periods is the *secondary dominant,* sometimes called the applied dominant.

The Secondary Dominant. This chord is characteristically a major triad or a dominant seventh chord in vertical structure. Minor triads and minor seventh chords may not function as secondary dominants. However, it is possible for the diminished triad and the diminished (or half-diminished) seventh chord to serve as secondary dominants where these chords function as incomplete dominant sevenths or ninths. Review Chapters XIX, XXVI, and Appendix B in Volume I (see below, Ex. I, A, (*e*) and (*f*)).

In addition to these characteristic vertical structural properties, there are horizontal considerations involving chord connections. The altered chord in question must have such a root relationship to an adjacent chord as can be expressed by the figures V and I.

This relationship may be indicated by the algebraic formula $a : b : : c : d$ (*a* is to *b* as *c* is to *d*), as follows:

	a	:	b	: :		c	:	d
C:	V^7 of IV	:	IV	: :	F :	V^7	:	I
C:	$_oV^9$ of II	:	II	: :	d :	$_oV^9$	:	I
C:	V of V	:	V	: :	G :	V	:	I
C:	V^7 of II	:	II	: :	d :	V^7	:	I

To illustrate further, let us suppose a D major chord to appear in a passage clearly in the key of C major. The D major chord resolves to (or is preceded by) a G major chord (V in C). The D chord here has a dominant (V) function with respect to the G chord. The unaltered D chord in C major (the regular II) is a minor triad and cannot have a dominant function. But the F♯ in the D major triad serves as a leading tone into G—there is an analogy to the leading tone in the key of G—and the D major triad is analogous to a V in the key of G major. The music does not modulate to G major unless there is a cadence in that key, carefully prepared and established. In this hypothetical example, then, one may say: $II^{♯3}$ is to V as V is to I; therefore $II^{♯3}$ should properly be analyzed as dominant of the dominant (V of V).

It should be evident that the term "dominant" has a relative as well as an absolute application, since it may refer to the *function* of a chord and is no longer limited to chords built on the 5th scale degree.

Let us summarize briefly:

(1) Structure: *triad* (major or diminished) or *seventh chord* (dominant, diminished, or half-diminished).

(2) Function of the secondary dominant: analogous to V.

(3) Function of the related chord: analogous to I. (It is possible for the chord to have a VI function, as in a deceptive cadence.)

(4) The raised tone in the secondary dominant (if there is only one alteration) will probably act as a leading tone into the diatonic tone of resolution.

(5) To qualify as a secondary dominant the chord must be a chromatically altered chord; i.e. it must include one or more tones that are a departure from the diatonic norm.

(6) The chord is figured V of V (*not* II$^{\#3}$), V^7 of IV (*not* I$^{7}_{\#3}$), etc.

(7) Any major or minor chord may have a related secondary dominant. Diminished and augmented triads are better excluded, since they cannot provide the tonic quality necessary in the resolution.

It must be emphasized that the great majority of all the altered chords in the music of Bach, Haydn, Mozart, Beethoven, Schumann, etc., are secondary dominants. Since this type of chord occurs with such great frequency, you should clearly understand it in order to recognize it at once when you analyze music. Your own writing will gain in color, in harmonic subtlety, and in linear fluidity as you incorporate these chords into your vocabulary.

Example I. Secondary Dominants and Their Relationship to Diatonic Harmonies.

A. Structural types.

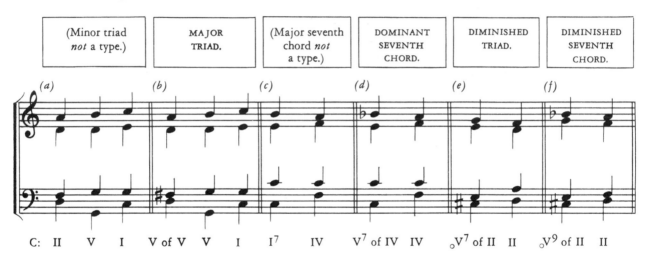

B. Analogues.

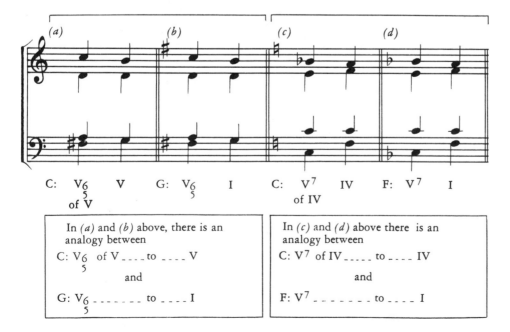

C. Related diatonic chord may appear before or after the secondary dominant.

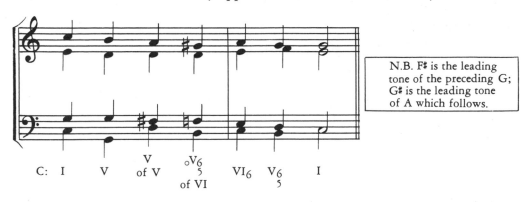

N.B. F♯ is the leading tone of the preceding G; G♯ is the leading tone of A which follows.

C: I   V   V   ᵒV₆   VI₆   V₆   I
              of V   ₅   ₅
                            of VI

D. Deceptive resolution of a secondary dominant.

C: I   V   V —⁷   III   I   V   I
              of V

In the above example III (E minor chord) is VI of the expected V (G major chord).   Thus, V⁷ of V is to III as V⁷ is to VI.

The Secondary II and IV. Chromatically altered chords usually need resolution. (An exception would be made in the case of the I with raised 3rd in the minor mode.) Altered chords seldom, then, have a tonic (rest) function. In addition to the dominant (V) function provided by the artificial leading tone (described above), it is possible for an altered chord to have a II or a IV function with respect to a temporary I. It is customary in this case for the II or IV to move to still another altered chord that will have a V function. The chord of resolution will thus be a center of gravity around which there may be one or several dependent satellite chords, comprising a distinct configuration or constellation.

Analysis along these lines helps one to distinguish between essential *diatonic* harmonies having *structural* significance on the one hand, and ornamental *chromatic,* embellishing chords that are *not structural* on the other hand.

Example II. The Secondary II and IV.

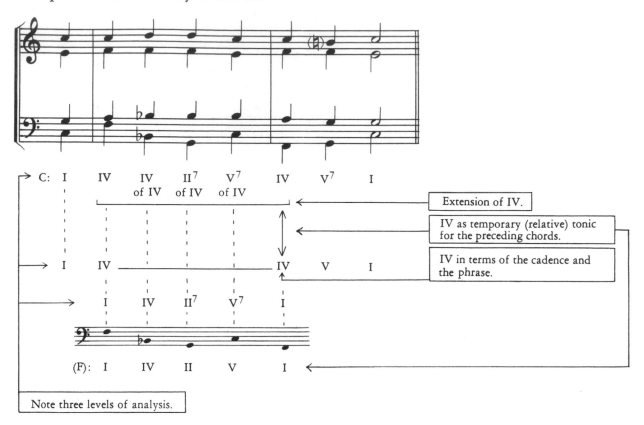

Guide to the Figuration of Altered Chords.

(1) Secondary V, II, or IV should be indicated as V, II, or IV of another chord, e.g.

    V of II   II of IV   IV of II

not: VI$^{\sharp 3}$ *not:* V$^{\flat 3}$ *not:* V$^{\flat 3}$

(2) Lowered or raised chord root is indicated by a flat or sharp before the roman numeral, e.g.

    $\sharp$IV $\flat$VII

If the alteration results in a secondary V, II, or IV, figure as in (1) above. Thus $\sharp$IV resolving to V might be more properly indicated as $_{\circ}$V^{7} of V resolving to V; $\flat$VII-III in minor should be designated as V of III followed by III.

(3) Alterations of chord-third, -fifth, or -seventh should be indicated at the upper right hand corner of the roman numeral, above and to the right of the inversion figures in the lower right-hand corner; thus:

    V$^{\flat 3}$ V$^{\flat\frac{7}{3}}$ V$^{\sharp 5}$ V$_{\frac{6}{5}}^{\sharp 5}$ V$^{\sharp 7}$ V$_{\frac{4}{2}}^{\sharp 7}$

SUGGESTED READING

Sessions, Ch. 8.
Piston, Ch. 14.
Mitchell, Ch. 17 (optional).

SUGGESTED EXERCISES

(a) Write solutions to problems selected from any of the above texts.

(b) Harmonize a soprano or bass line (two phrases) of one of the Bach chorales. Use several secondary dominants.

(c) Dictation of phrases employing secondary dominants.

(d) Play at the keyboard:

$$
\begin{array}{ccccccccc}
\text{I} & \text{V} & \text{V} & \text{I} & & \text{I} & \text{V}_6 & \text{I}_6^4 & \text{V} & \text{I} \\
 & \text{of V} & & & & & \text{of V} & & &
\end{array}
$$

$$
\begin{array}{ccccccccc}
\text{I} & \text{V}_5^6 & \text{V}^{-7} & \text{I} & & \text{I} & \text{IV} & \text{V} & \text{II} & \text{V} & \text{I} \\
 & \text{of V} & & & & & \text{of II} & \text{of II} & & &
\end{array}
$$

(e) Work out at the piano the formulas prescribed at the end of Chapter 14 in Piston, op. cit.

(f) Sing, using numbers, then syllables. Analyze for secondary dominant implications.

IV

The Harmonic Structure of the Phrase

We turn again to the subject of phrase construction. The phrase is the smallest musical structure that can be regarded as having a reasonable measure of completeness, and it culminates in some form of cadence (resting point) as we have already observed in previous chapters (see Vol. I, Ch. V, XIII, XVII, and XXVII).

Harmonic Rhythm. The rate of change of harmonies is called harmonic rhythm. The idea of harmonic rhythm was suggested in Volume I, Chapter XIII, Exercise (a). In that illustration there are two measures of I (tonic) followed by one measure of V (dominant), another of I, and one measure each of IV, I, V, and I. The harmonic rhythm of this eight-measure example could be indicated as illustrated in Example I.

Example I. The Harmonic Rhythm of Example (a), Volume I, Chapter XIII.

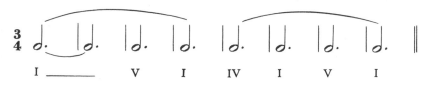

I _____ V I IV I V I

N.B. The rate of harmonic change is regular: one chord per measure, except for mm. 1-2 which are a single harmony.

This subject has been covered in some detail in Piston, Chapter 5. Note there the author's analysis of his Examples 78–80, and the great contrast between Examples 85 and 86. The same subject is discussed under the title "Harmonic Elaboration" in Sessions, Chapter VII, section 4. Read both these texts carefully and be sure you understand each of the illustrations. Note particularly the Beethoven String Quartet illustration and the excerpt from the "Eroica" Symphony (figs. 129–30) in Sessions, observing the relationship between the original (in piano reduced score) and the schematic reduction (see also Appendix, Ex. F, at the end of this volume).

Chord Groups. The subject of chord groups was introduced in Volume I, Chapter XVII and illustrated there in Example I. In that example we can observe three levels of organization or grouping:

(1) the level of the measure, in which four chords are related;
(2) the level of the phrase, which here comprises two of the smaller groups; and
(3) the entire illustration, which is a combination of phrases.

A more extended illustration would have an even greater number of levels of organization.

———

To illustrate further harmonic rhythm and chord groups, we have diagrammed below measures 1–8 of the Scarlatti example in the Appendix (Ex. C) at the end of this volume. Discuss the diagram in class, relating each element to the music on the score page. Analyze the balance of the work in similar fashion.

Example II. Diagram of Scarlatti Sonata Excerpt (Appendix, Ex. C, measures 1–8).

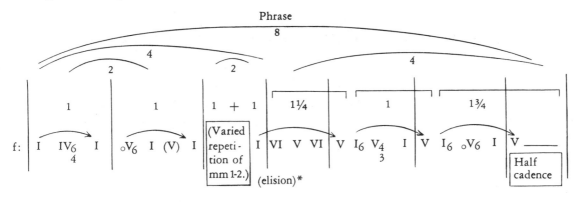

Harmonic tension and resolution. Just as there are alternations of strong, medium, and weak pulses in meter, so chords that *need* resolution (are relatively unstable) alternate with others that *are* resolutions (are more stable).

In the Scarlatti example just analyzed, the IV_4^6 (meas. one) is unstable and resolves back to I. Note, however, that the chord of resolution is on the fourth beat, a weak beat in the measure. In measure two there are two groups of V-I, with the resolutions again falling on the weak beats. These two measures are repeated. At the end of measure four there is an *elision** caused by the tied note over the bar line: the left hand, on the fourth beat, concludes the preceding phrase while the right hand, on the same beat, initiates the next phrase. The next group of chords resolves to a V on the strong first beat of measure six. Then there are two more groups each of which progresses to a V on a strong beat. The last V sounds for a complete measure and has, as a result, considerable weight.

The emphasis on I chords on weak beats as chords of resolution in the first four measures is in striking contrast to the emphasis on V chords on strong beats in the second four measures. The chord groups close on weak beats at first and then on strong beats. The strong I chords on weak beats balance the weaker V chords that appear on strong beats.

While on the subject of balance, note further: (a) the slightly asymmetrical 4 + 4 measure groups, (b) the contrast of four measures of I endings with four measures of V endings; (c) the almost consistent use of four chords in each small group.

SUGGESTED READING

Piston, Ch. 5.
Sessions, Ch. 7, Sect. 4.

————

SUGGESTED EXERCISES

(a) Write two or three phrases, each six to eight measures in length, illustrating common chord modulation to a closely related key. Employ different harmonic rhythms and chord groupings in each. Analyze them to show the tension-resolution principles discussed and illustrated above. Each example should have at least one secondary dominant chord.

————

*Overlapping or dovetailing of structural units.

(b) Improvise at the piano an accompaniment for the following melody. Use a few secondary dominants.

(c) Harmonize the following bass. Discuss the chord groups and the modulation process employed.

(d) Sing (b) and (c) above, using syllables, then numbers.

(e) Sing modulating chorale melodies. Discuss each.

(f) Dictation of modulating and nonmodulating melodies and harmonized chorales. There should be a few secondary dominants in each.

V

The Period

After the phrase the period is the next larger structure in the hierarchy of musical forms. It is a combination and balance of related phrases. A rigid definition or description of a period is difficult, if not impossible, and in the analysis of music one may not always be able to locate or isolate period form at once, or distinguish it from similar but slightly different structures.

The period is a further manifestation of the principle of alternating tension and resolution (already noted in connection with the subject of nonharmonic tones, chord groups, etc.). It is a swinging of the rhythmic pendulum over a larger canvas. The tension occurs in the first phrase (the *antecedent* phrase), sometimes regarded as analogous to a question. The resolution is accomplished in the second phrase (the *consequent* phrase) which would thus be like an answer to the previous question.

There is probably an inexhaustable list of possible shapes that periods may assume, but a consideration of some of the more familiar types and characteristics may prove helpful.

Number of Phrases. Most frequently there are two phrases, one antecedent and one consequent, as described above. However, it is possible to have three and even four phrases combine to make a single period, in which case there will be either:

(1) antecedent—antecedent—consequent,

(2) antecedent—consequent—consequent, or

(3) antecedent—antecedent—consequent—consequent.

Note that all of the above antecedent phrases appear before the consequent phrases. However, if one finds.

(4) antecedent—consequent—antecedent—consequent:

this arrangement should be likened to ‖: antecedent—consequent :‖ and should be thought of as comprising a *repeated period*. In a repeated period the first antecedent-consequent group is repeated exactly (minor embellishments permitted). In a *double period* the second of the two consequent phrases has a stronger cadence than the first consequent and is thus more conclusive, and a more complex structure than the repeated period results, thus:

(5) antecedent—CONSEQUENT—antecedent—CONSEQUENT.

Balance of Cadences. A wide range of possibilities exists, and the simplest general rule is that the antecedent phrase will end with a weaker cadence than the consequent. Some of the more familiar types of relationships or pairs are shown in Example I below.

Example I. Typical Cadential Relationships.

	Antecedent Phrase Closes with:	Consequent Phrase Closes with:
(a)	Half cadence*	Perfect authentic cadence*
(b)	Half cadence	Imperfect authentic cadence*
(c)	Imperfect authentic cadence	Perfect authentic cadence
(d)	Half cadence in a related key	Authentic cadence in the same related key
(e)	Half cadence in a related key	Authentic cadence in the tonic key
(f)	Imperfect authentic cadence in the tonic, weakened by elision or other means	Half cadence in a related key, strengthened by extension

> Any one of these consequent phrases *may* be in another (usually closely related) key.

The factors that determine the *strength* of a cadence are:

(1) the cadence type (perfect is stronger than imperfect, etc.);

(2) the key (the tonic is stronger than a related key);

(3) rhythmic weight (first beat is stronger than second or third);

(4) associated textural and/or dynamic changes (greater changes are generally associated with stronger cadences);

(5) duration (the longer the cadential chord the stronger it is).

Thematic Relationship Possibilities. The three typical ways of relating the consequent phrase to the antecedent phrase are as follows:

(1) Parallel Construction. This terms applies when the antecedent and consequent phrases begin with the same materials. It is of course essential that the cadences be different and that the melodic closes be different, otherwise (if the two phrases were identical) one would have only a repeated phrase and not a period. Ornamental embellishments in a second phrase otherwise like a first phrase are insufficient to establish the consequent quality: there must be differences in both the melodic and the harmonic structure somewhere in (generally at the close of) the consequent phrase (see Ex. II).

(2) Sequential Construction. The beginning of the consequent phrase may have melodic and harmonic materials that correspond to (have the same shape as) the opening of the antecedent phrase but occur on different scale degrees or in another key. This is a sequential relationship. Sequence always involves immediate repetition on other scale degrees: the octave is not a different scale degree; therefore, repetition at the octave is not sequence but an example of variation (see Ex. III).

---

* See Vol. I, Ch. XIII, Ex. I, for definition and illustration of these terms.

(3) Contrasting Construction. The beginnings of the antecedent and consequent phrases may employ different melodic materials. It is of no concern here whether the cadences or phrase endings are similar or different, but the second cadence should still be the stronger of the two. Since the phrases are not related melodically, it is common for them to be unified either by

(a) a consistent accompaniment texture or figure, or

(b) a consistent rhythmic motive in the melody (see Ex. IV).

Where there is more than one antecedent or consequent phrase, as in Example IV, the two paired phrases (double antecedent or double consequent) will be either very closely related to each other, or perhaps exactly the same, or identical but for slight differences at the cadence. The uncoupled (single) phrase in a three-phrase period must be less similar to either of the paired phrases than the two paired phrases are to each other.

Number of Measures. There is a widely accepted notion that musical phrases must be (or usually are) four measures long. This is no more true than that sentences have eight words, that all poetic lines are iambic pentameter, or that living rooms must be 12' x 16'. Periods may be composed of phrases of various lengths, and the balancing phrases are *not necessarily* symmetrical or identical in size. A consequent phrase may be extended in order to secure greater weight at the cadence, especially in the final phrase of a three- or four-phrase period, or at the end of a composition to create a feeling of greater rest and finality. Periods usually are not composed of long, rambling phrases: the phrase components are likely to be terse, declaratory, direct, and without the developmental elements associated with the looser and less definite chain phrases.*

A number of typical period forms and antecedent-consequent relationships are illustrated below in Examples II, III, and IV.

---

* Not to be confused with the period are (1) the *chain phrase,* a long, rambling, developmental phrase with a single cadence at the close (as in Appendix, Ex. E); and (2) the *chain of phrases,* a loosely associated group of related phrases each with its own cadence, the last of which is the strongest (see Appendix, Ex. A).

Example II. Brahms, Variations on a Theme by Joseph Haydn. The Opening Measures (Period Form).

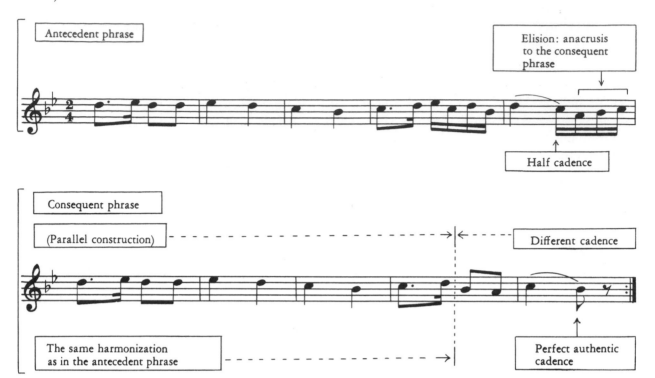

Appoggiatura-like chords fall on the first beat of measures 5 and 10, causing the phrase and cadence to close on the (weaker) second beat of the measure ("feminine cadence").

Since the period is played twice it may be regarded as a "repeated period." Compare Ex. III which is a "double period" because there is greater weight at the end of the second period than at the first ending (end of the first period). This is caused by the stopping of the bass line and the avoidance of the seventh in the V chord.

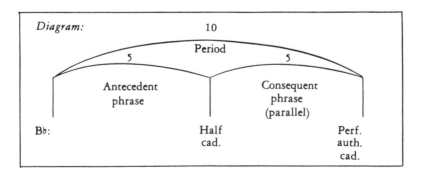

Example III. Mendelssohn, Song Without Words No. 14. The Opening Measures (Double Period).

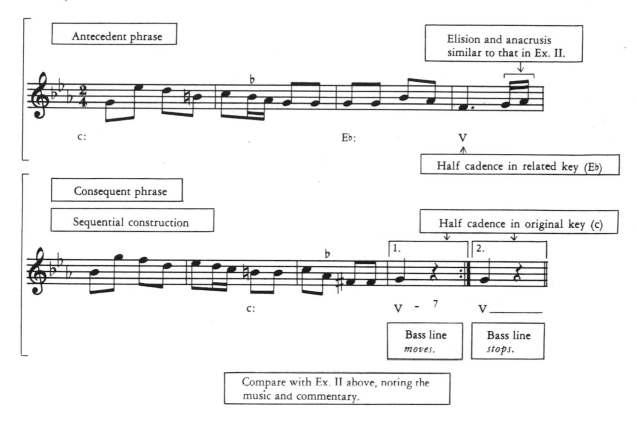

Example IV. Beethoven, Symphony No. 7, Second Movement. The Opening Measures (Three-Phrase Period).

Antecedent phrase (begins in a minor).

Imperfect authentic cadence in the related key of C major.

a: C: I

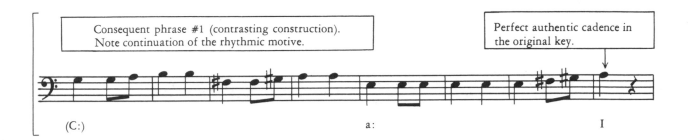

Consequent phrase #1 (contrasting construction). Note continuation of the rhythmic motive.

Perfect authentic cadence in the original key.

(C:)   a: I

Consequent phrase #2 (repetition of first consequent phrase).

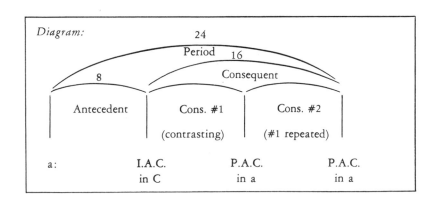

Diagram:

SUGGESTED EXERCISES

(a) Analyze selected period forms in Mozart Piano Sonatas. Compare these with representative examples of the two-phrase units (set off by double-bar and repeat sign) that open many of the Bach chorales.

(b) Write diagrammatic sketches of at least six possible period forms, showing a variety of keys, phrase lengths, number of phrases, cadential types, degrees of rhythmic weight at the cadences, and so forth. Choose *two* of these (using similar thematic materials) and compose music corresponding to the diagrams.

(c) Identify by ear various types of phrase and period structure. These may be performed by the instructor at the piano, or recordings may be used.

(d) Improvise at the keyboard each of the three types of consequent phrase (parallel, sequential, contrasting), using the following phrase as an antecedent. At least one of them should modulate to a closely related key. Suggestion: begin the sequential consequent phrase on the V chord, and end on I; the contrasting consequent phrase should be related somehow to the antecedent phrase, e.g. by an accompaniment that is similar in texture and rhythm.

(e) Make a diagram of Example III above, and of Example I in the Appendix, measures 1–8

The Harmonic Structure of Phrases and Periods

Analysis. Continue the study of modulation, the secondary dominant (and the secondary II and IV), and phrase and period structure in the works of different composers. Examine carefully some of the examples quoted at the end of this volume, in the Appendix. Use the questions suggested there as a basis for study and class discussion.

See also opening phrase and period structures in many of the Mozart sonatas, especially in the slow movements, and minuets and trios. Analyze Bach chorale phrases in similar fashion, comparing the styles and techniques of the two composers.

Make diagrams of these phrases and periods, following the models suggested in previous chapters.

Composition. Practice writing short phrases and periods. Make a preliminary diagram of the structural elements, and then write corresponding music. Minor details of the diagram may be altered as the composition progresses.

One useful type of exercise is the composition of several different continuations from a given beginning. You should practice writing in the piano style of Mozart as well as in the four-voice chorale style of Bach. Analyze everything you write: critical evaluation is just as important for your musical growth as the creative act.

Supplementary Exercises

(a) Dictation of phrases and periods involving common chord modulation, secondary dominants, a variety of cadential forms.

(b) Practice at the keyboard the realization of figured and unfigured chorale melodies.

(c) Sing the following melody, following the procedure suggested in Chapter I, Exercise (a).

Chromatically Altered Chords (Part Two)

In addition to the secondary dominant and related forms already discussed in Chapter III, there are a number of other familiar and useful types of chromatically altered chords. The most important of these are discussed in the paragraphs below.

The Neapolitan Sixth Chord. This term, the origin of which is obscure, refers to the first inversion of a major triad whose root is the lowered supertonic ($\flat$II$_6$). It appears most commonly in the minor mode where only the root need be chromatically changed. In the less frequent major mode usage, both the root and the fifth of the triad are lowered.

The chord may appear in root position ($\flat$II), but characteristically appears in first inversion—hence the name *sixth chord.* As in the unaltered II$_6$, the third of the chord (which is in the bass) suggests the root of the IV chord. The II$_6$ and the Neapolitan sixth chord are thus strongly related to the IV chord, and in many cases serve as substitutes for IV.

The second inversion of the Neapolitan chord is possible, but extremely rare. Its resolution is governed not only by the same factors that apply to the root position and first inversion of the chord, but also by the considerations that limit all six-four chords.

Like the unaltered II or IV, the Neapolitan sixth chord (N6) usually progresses to the V, or to the I$_6^4$ which in turn resolves to V, especially at a cadence. It is further possible for a chord with a Neapolitan sixth function to resolve to a secondary dominant as in Example I (*c*). In this case the "$\flat$II" should be related to the chord that is a temporary tonic (the chord being embellished by the secondary dominant) rather than related to the tonic of the key.

Example I. The Neapolitan Sixth Chord (N6 or $\flat$II$_6$).

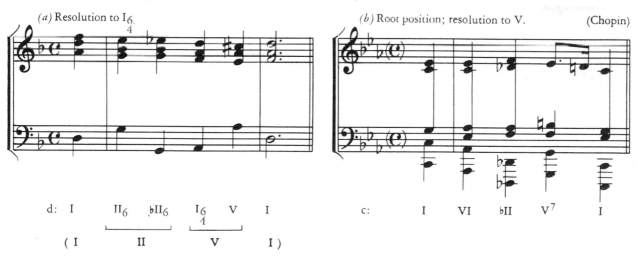

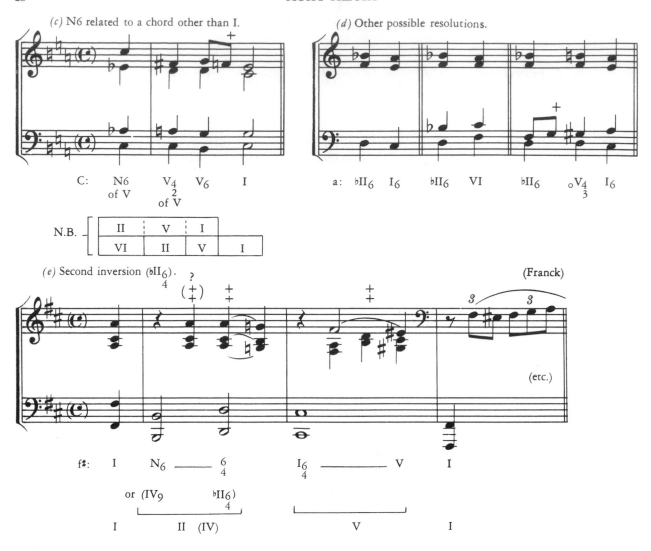

(c) N6 related to a chord other than I.

C: N6   V4   V6   I
      of V   2
             of V

(d) Other possible resolutions.

a: ♭II6   I6   ♭II6   VI   ♭II6   °V4   I6
                                       3

N.B.

II	V	I
VI	II	V	I

(e) Second inversion (♭II6).
                4

(Franck)

(etc.)

f♯:   I   N6 ———— 6   I6 ———————— V   I
                   4   4

or (IV9   ♭II6)
                 4

I   II (IV)   V   I

The Augmented Sixth Chords. This collective title refers to a family of chords which have in common the interval of the augmented sixth (or, somewhat less commonly, the inversion of that interval—the diminished third). They characteristically have a *subdominant function* (having as a root either ♯IV, II, or ♯II) and usually resolve to a chord having a *dominant* function. There are, of course, irregular or less common resolutions which may be accounted for by considerations involving the context. The three most familiar types of augmented sixth chord are the so-called Italian sixth (not to be confused with the Neapolitan sixth chord), the German sixth, and the French sixth.

The *Italian sixth* is the only triad of the three—the others are seventh chords. It is the enharmonic equivalent of a dominant seventh whose fifth is omitted, though in structure and spelling it is always a triad. The *German sixth* is the enharmonic equivalent of a complete dominant seventh chord (with the fifth). There are two ways of spelling this chord, as shown in Example II, A, below. The *French sixth* is somewhat more dissonant in character, owing to the greater emphasis upon the interval of the minor seventh (or its enharmonic equivalent) and its inversion, the major second. It does *not* sound like an enharmonic dominant seventh chord.

Because of the ambiguity of these chords in *sound,* they are very useful as modulatory agents, as "common" or "pivot" chords (see Ch. XVIII below).

The augmented sixth chords usually resolve in such a manner that the interval of the augmented sixth expands by stepwise contrary motion to the interval of an octave (or the diminished third or tenth will resolve by contraction stepwise to a unison or octave). The doubled tone in the resolution is characteristically the root of the chord of resolution (normally V). The V may be preceded, of course, by an embellishing I_4^6 in the same manner as indicated in Example I (*a*) and (*e*) above.

Example II. The Augmented Sixth Chords, (A6).

A. The typical forms, shown in the key of C.

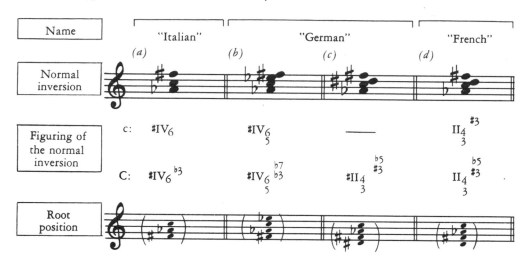

B. The Italian sixth, and suggested resolutions.

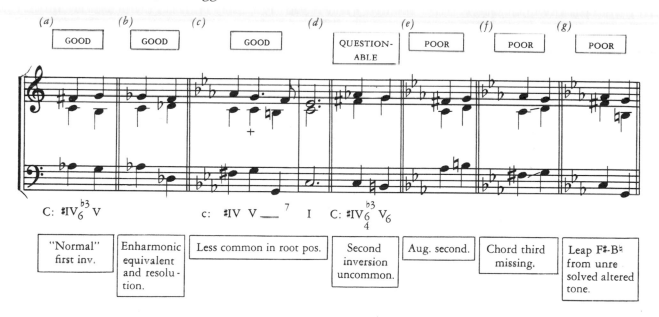

C. The German sixth and suggested resolutions.

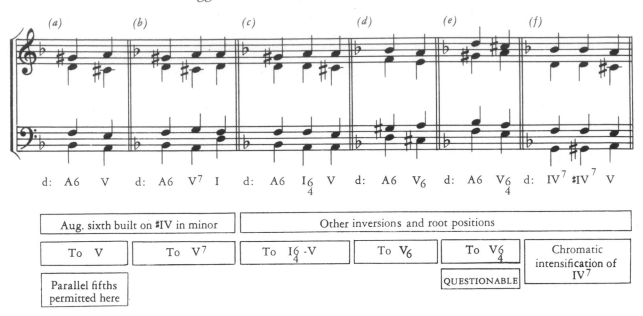

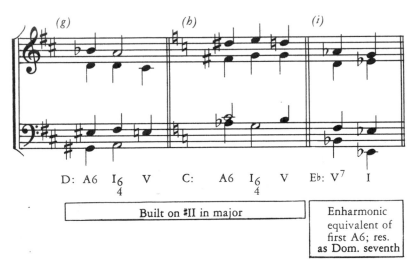

D. The French sixth and suggested resolutions.

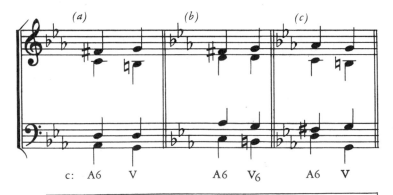

N.B. Leap of a fifth in the bass, tripled root in the chord of
resolution in (c).　　Substitute for V^7 of V (fifth of V^7 is
lowered).　　Compare Ex. III below.

Rather exceptionally, the interval of the augmented sixth (or diminished third) resolves into an octave (or unison) which is not the doubled root of the V chord (or doubled fifth of the attendant I_6^4), but a *doubled third.* This is true in the case of the V[7] with ♯5. Note that this chord is *dominant* in function, not subdominant, and hence rather distinct and different from the "true" augmented sixth chord. The V[7] with ♯5 resolves to a I chord rather than a V, and the augmented or diminished interval resolves to a doubled chord-*third* in the I chord (see Ex. III (*a*) below).

The V[7] with ♭5 resembles the French sixth in sound, contains the augmented sixth (or diminished third) interval, and it, too, is dominant in function. The augmented or diminished interval resolves to the doubled *root* of the I chord (see Ex. III (*b*) below).

Example III. The $V_{\sharp5}^{7}$ and the $V_{\flat5}^{7}$.

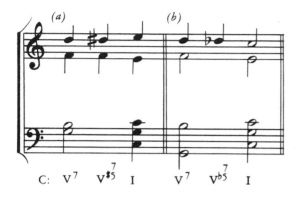

The augmented sixth chords are generally useful in all inversions (except the Italian sixth, which is questionable as a six-four chord). In the seventh chords none of the four tones should be omitted. The Italian sixth is to be expected in a three-voice texture, and when used in four-part writing should have its chord-fifth doubled. Avoid doubling either tone of the "sensitive" augmented sixth interval.

The Picardy Third (I[♯3]). This term is used to describe the raised (major) third in the tonic triad sometimes used in the final chord of a work otherwise in the minor mode (see Ex. 74, Ch. 4 in Piston, op. cit.). It does not affect the sense of tonality of the work, but it has an acoustical effect and a dramatic and expressive function that is useful in many situations. Occasionally the idea of the Picardy third ("tierce de Picardie") is applied to the end of a major section or division of a larger form.

Note, in review, that the Picardy third has a *tonic* function, the Neapolitan and augmented sixth chords have a *subdominant* function, and the secondary dominants have (as the name indicates) a *dominant* function.

SUGGESTED READING

Sessions, Ch. 12, sect. 2.
Piston, Ch. 23–4. Note especially the numerous illustrations and exercises.

SUGGESTED EXERCISES

(a) Write six examples of each type of augmented sixth chord, using a variety of keys, major and minor, different inversions, and so forth, resolving each.

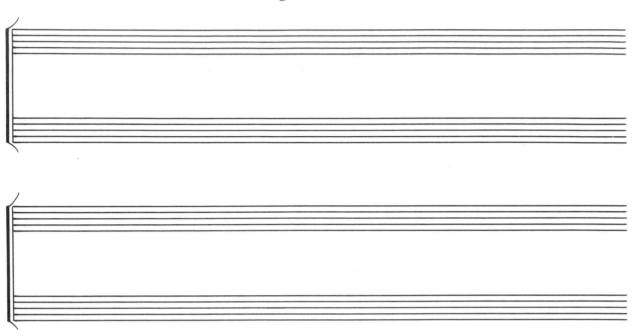

(b) Problems in the use of N6 and A6 chords (to be worked out in class).

    (1) *Question:* Where can the A6 and the N6 be used? *Answer:* The A6 may be used to harmonize the scale degrees 1, 2, ♯2, ♭3, ♯4, and ♭6. The N6 may be used to harmonize ♭2, 4, or ♭6. *Question:* How do they resolve? *Answer:* Generally to the V or I₆; the V may be a secondary dominant.

    (2) *Question:* How does one "find" the A6 chord? *Answer:* (1) Locate the A6 (or diminished third) *interval,* usually between scale degrees ♭6 and ♯4; (2) see if it can be properly resolved (usually ♭6-5, ♯4-5); (3) locate the chord root (♯IV, II, or ♯II), choosing the tone that best suits the context; (4) locate the chord third, fifth (and seventh as needed).

    (3) *Question:* How can an A6 resolve to a secondary V? *Answer:* Follow above procedures. However, the ♯4 and ♭6 of the A6 and the 5 (V) of the resolution should be figured in relation to a chord *other* than the tonic. See the fourth beat of measure two in Exercise c (2) below.

(c) Problems in using the N6 and A6 chords (to be worked out individually).

    (1) Use the A6 chord where indicated:

C: I   A6   I₆/₄   V

(2) Use A6 and N6 as indicated:

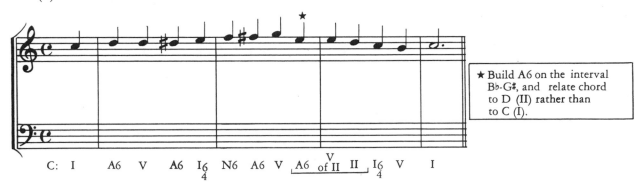

★ Build A6 on the interval
Bb-G♯, and relate chord
to D (II) rather than
to C (I).

C: I   A6   V   A6   I$_6^4$ N6   A6   V   A6 of II   II   I$_6^4$ V   I

(d) Play in several keys, major and minor:

I   A6   I$_6^4$ V   I

I   A6   V^7 I

I   N6   V^{-7} I

I   II$_6$ N6   I$_6^4$ V^{-7} I

(e) Sing at sight. Use syllables, then numbers:

(f) Harmonize (e) at the keyboard. The melody should be transposed up an octave.

(g) Locate all the secondary dominants, Neapolitan and augmented sixth chords in Examples D, E, and F of the Appendix.

(h) Dictation of examples involving N6 and A6 chords.

Chromatically Altered Chords (Part Three)

Continue the analysis, writing, and discussion of Neapolitan sixth and augmented sixth chords. Examine the use of these chords in the musical literature, as suggested by the instructor. Neapolitan sixths may be seen in the Mozart examples in the Appendix, augmented sixths in the examples by Schubert and Beethoven (second half). Study the context in which these chords appear, their introduction and resolution; also matters of doubling, voice leading; location in the phrase, and so forth.

Exercises devised by the instructor should be worked out by the class at the blackboard first, and then individually in home assignments.

SUGGESTED EXERCISES

(a) Answer the questions pertaining to Examples D, E, F, and G in the Appendix.

(b) Harmonize the four-measure melody of Exercise c(2), Chapter VII, using it as a bass line. Follow the general harmonic plan as given, using inversions of suggested chords as necessary.

(c) Sing at sight:

(d) Harmonize (c) above, using N6 and A6 chords where appropriate. There should be one chord per measure for the most part, with occasional changes in the harmonic rhythm.

(e) Improvise a keyboard harmonization of the following, using N6, A6, or Picardy third where indicated:

(f) Dictation, with emphasis on A6 and N6 chords.

IX

Exercises in Analysis

In the study of the language of music we must learn more than vocabulary. As with verbal expression, one must become acquainted with idioms, with syntactical usage, and with the appropriateness of words to a given context.

The previous chapters were largely concerned with the enlargement of your harmonic vocabulary. It will take some time to learn to use these terms idiomatically and with a sense of style. It is important to use them with consistency and with logic, and (perhaps most important to the beginning student) not to over-indulge or use them excessively.

Considerable time should be devoted to the further study (through analysis, diagramming, and reduction) of Bach chorales, sections of Mozart sonatas, and the examples in the Appendix at the end of this volume. Be particularly alert to methods of modulation, to the use of altered chords, and to the harmonic structure of phrases and phrase groups.

You will notice, for example, that the number of secondary dominants is greater than the combined number of all other forms of altered chords. Observe the differences in harmonic rhythm, in texture, and in principles of phrase-period balance in the various composers. In comparing chorale style with keyboard style note the comparative rapidity of the harmonic rhythm in the former, and the frequent tendency toward elaboration and extension in the latter.

Harmonic analyses should be made directly under the music analyzed or on a separate sheet. The making of diagrams and schematic reductions should be practiced in class, and then individually in home assignments.

SUPPLEMENTARY EXERCISES

(a) Assigned melodies are to be prepared for keyboard harmonization. They should involve common chord modulation problems, at least one or two chromatically altered tones, and a few tones to be treated as nonharmonic tones. Students should learn how to find, how to play with proper doubling and spacing, and how to resolve the various types of altered chords discussed to date.

(b) Dictation of examples, using secondary dominants, Neapolitan sixth and augmented sixth chords, and the Picardy third. The examples should be short at first until recognition of chord sound and function is achieved quickly and easily; longer examples may follow.

(c) Sight singing of modulating melodies, and of melodic lines that imply altered chords.

X

Exercise in Composition

Write a period of three or four phrases, altogether about 16–24 measures in length. A diagram of your own specifications should accompany the musical example. Show the key, modulation plan, cadence types, harmonic structure, chord groups, and so forth. Use chorale or keyboard style. Strive for unity of style and texture, without monotony or excessive repetition and squareness. Achieve a melodic line that has direction and curve, and a bass line that is appropriate to it.

Try to use (without excess) several nonharmonic tones, labeling each, and a few altered chords. The final result should be musical, and only secondarily an illustration of vocabulary or technique. Make the means truly serve the ends. Play the music many times, until you are sure it is as perfect as you can make it. If possible, write away from the keyboard, using the latter only to check your results; this will help to strengthen your inner ear and enable you gradually to work with greater ease and rapidity.

Since music exists so very much in time, work out a few basic lines (rhythm, soprano, bass, harmonic structure), gradually adding details. Do not try to write melody, harmony, and rhythm simultaneously. Quickly project an objective in at least one of these areas, and then bridge the gap with all the imagination and resources you can command. The creative impulse must be free and bold in gesture, and not inhibited by simultaneous criticism. Let your critical faculty examine quite objectively the results of your artistic impulse, but only after a measureable quantity of product has been created.

Above all, don't let your mind become congested with conflicting ideas. If you reach an impasse, continue at work for a while, but if you still make no progress, leave your sketches and engage in a completely different activity (preferably physical exercise!), returning later with fresh impulses and a clearer head.

SUPPLEMENTARY EXERCISES

(a) Improvise at the keyboard short phrases that modulate:

(1) From G to D	(7) From b to D
(2) . . . . . . to e	(8) . . . . . . to e
(3) . . . . . . to C	(9) . . . . . . to G
(4) . . . . . . to A	(10) . . . . . . to f♯
(5) . . . . . . to f♯	(11) . . . . . . to A
(6) . . . . . . to b	(12) . . . . . . to E

(b) Dictation as in Chapter IX. The examples should be longer, perhaps more complex rhythmically, and should involve more nonharmonic tones.

(c) Sight singing of modulating melodies and of nonmodulating melodies that involve chromatically altered tones.

The Dominant Ninth Chord

Before studying the materials of this chapter, the student is urged to read Chapter 16 in Mitchell and Chapter 18 in Piston, examining the exercises, schematic illustrations, and quotations from the musical literature. It would be well to make an outline of the principal points stressed by each author. List separately the matters on which they agree and disagree.

Example I. The Dominant Ninth Chord: Figuration of Root Position and the Inversions.

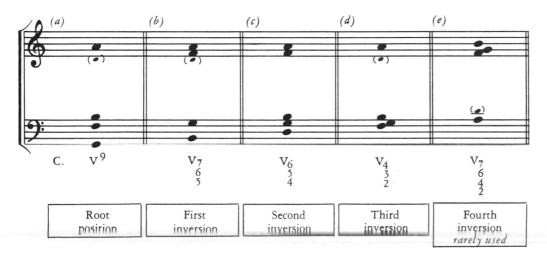

Usage Principles. The following general principles govern the construction and resolution of ninth chords generally, and dominant ninths chords in particular:

(1) Root position is preferred; first inversion is next most common; second and third inversions are less common; fourth inversion is rare.

(2) The chord-ninth is best placed in the soprano (upper) voice.

(3) The root should be as low as possible, and below the ninth.

(4) Chord spacing should emphasize thirds and sixths; avoid overemphasis of intervals of the second.

(5) V^9 is much more frequently used than are nondominant ninths.

(6) The chord-fifth may be omitted (except, of course, in the second inversion; here the third is omitted). The seventh is characteristically present. If the root is absent, the chord is an $_{o}V^9$.

(7) Chord-sevenths and -ninths both resolve down stepwise normally—in the next chord, often together in parallel thirds, sometimes independently. Occasionally the resolution of the chord-ninth is understood (implicit) in the harmony rather than explicit in the expected voice—though the seventh in the chord will still be expected to resolve in the customary fashion. The resolution of the chord-ninth, like that of the chord-seventh, may be delayed, transferred to another voice, or subject to ornamentation and decoration.

Example II. Illustrations of the Usage Principles.

$$\text{C: IV} \quad \text{V}^9 \quad \text{I} \quad \text{II}^7 \quad \text{V}^9 \quad \text{V}^6_{5\,4} \quad \text{I}_6 \quad \text{V}^9 \quad \text{V}^4_{3\,2} \quad \text{I} \quad \text{I} \quad \text{V}_{7\,6\,5} \quad \text{I} \quad \text{I}_6 \quad \text{IV} \quad \text{V}_{7\,6\,4} \quad \text{I}_{6\,4} \quad \text{V}^{7-9-7} \quad \text{I}$$

SUGGESTED READING

Mitchell, Ch. 16.
Piston, Ch. 18.

———

SUGGESTED EXERCISES

(a) Analyze the Chopin mazurka, Example I in the Appendix, noting particularly the use of ninth chords.

(b) Write (in four-part harmony) single, unconnected, root position dominant ninth chords above the given bass and below the given soprano notes.

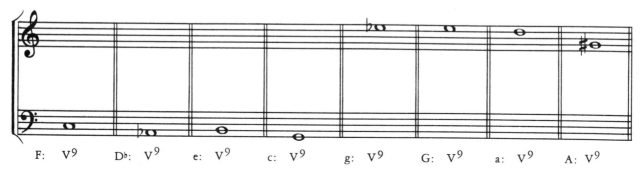

$$\text{F: V}^9 \qquad \text{D}\flat\text{: V}^9 \qquad \text{e: V}^9 \qquad \text{c: V}^9 \qquad \text{g: V}^9 \qquad \text{G: V}^9 \qquad \text{a: V}^9 \qquad \text{A: V}^9$$

(c) Write several of the above chords in first, second, and third inversion. Supply the appropriate figuration for each.

---

* The suspended C has a long-delayed resolution. When it finally resolves to the B in the last measure the underlying harmony has moved ahead to the I chord. The effect of the double appoggiatura is to perpetuate, almost as another suspension, the sense of the previous V chord.

(d) Repeat exercises (b) and (c) above, but rearrange the spacing of the chords and provide each with a suitable resolution. (Use separate sheet of paper.)

(e) Provide a written harmonization for the following, using a few dominant ninth chords in each example.

(f) Play at the piano in several keys:

(1) I V^9 I

(2) I IV II^7 V^9 I

(3) I IV V^9 I

(4) I V V$_{\substack{7\\6\\5}}$ I

(g) Dictation of examples that include several dominant ninth chords.

XII

Harmonic Texture

Since much of the study of harmony involves four-part writing, the student may be misled into thinking that four-part harmony is "normal" or characteristic of most music. A quick glance at the literature of music should be enough to dispel this notion. Four-part harmony is most useful in teaching harmonic principles, and it may even be thought of as assumed or understood in much music that is in either more or fewer voices. But the consistent use of four parts is found in very little music other than in the chorale (or hymn tune) style. Even a four-voice fugue is in three parts much of the time, as one voice or another has a few measures rest.

The student should acquire practice in both the analysis and the writing of music in one-, two-, and three-voice texture, and in keyboard style as well as in four voices. For *three-voice* texture see sections of many of the Mozart piano sonatas, and the three-voice inventions (sinfonias) and the French and English suites for piano by Bach. *Two-voice* writing may be found in many of the sonatas of Scarlatti, movements of the above-mentioned suites of Bach, and the latter's two-voice inventions; see also sections of movements of Mozart piano sonatas. The best examples of single-line or *one-voice* texture may be found in the partitas and sonatas for unaccompanied violin by Bach (see Appendix, Ex. B, part 2), where the single line may suggest several lines or outline a progression of well-defined chords. This is quite unlike the monophonic plainchant (Gregorian chant) which has no harmonic orientation.* A single line accompaniment to a well-defined melody may take the form of a broken chord, as in an Alberti bass.† *Keyboard style* embraces a great many kinds of texture, and may include the above-mentioned Alberti bass. In a sense it is no "style" at all, since it is so varied. It may involve idiomatic figuration (arpeggios, etc.), a freedom from consistent use of any set number of voices and a consequent frequent appearance and disappearance of textural lines, octave doubling, etc. Several lines may occasionally merge (by assuming unison doubling) into a smaller number of lines. Expected harmonic tones may be omitted as acoustically or psychologically "understood."

The examples in the Appendix at the end of this volume should be examined, and their use of textures compared.

SUGGESTED EXERCISES

(a) Write four short compositions, each one phrase in length, based on the following harmonic scheme:

(Pivot)

d: I VI IV$^{(7)}$ A6 V

e: IV$^{\sharp 3}$ N6‡ V I$^{\sharp 3}$ N6 A6 I$_6^4$ V^{-7} I

As an alternative, one may plan this as a two- or three-phrase period, with the d:V serving as a half cadence for the antecedent phrase.

(b) Prepare one or more of the figured chorales at the back of the Riemenschneider edition of the Bach chorales (see the Suggested Supplementary Materials listed on p. vii) as follows:

(1) Play in three-part harmony, keeping the original soprano and bass lines.

(2) Play in three-part harmony, keeping only the soprano line; improvise a new bass line.

---

*See Vol. I: Ch. I, Ex. I(*a*); and Ch. V, Ex. I(*a*).

† See articles on this term in *Grove's Dictionary of Music and Musicians* (Eric Blom, ed.), 5th ed., St. Martin's Press, Inc., New York, 1955; and in Willi Apel, *Harvard Dictionary of Music,* Harvard University Press, Cambridge (Mass.), 1944.

‡ Use in root position.

(3) Play in two-part harmony, using the original bass line; improvise a new soprano line.

(4) Play in four-part harmony, up to a given point (perhaps a fermata); then improvise a new continuation, abandoning the original soprano and bass lines. Modulate to another key through a common chord, closing with the following cadence:

A6 I_6^4 V^{-7} I.

(c) Dictation of examples in two to five voices and in keyboard style. Emphasis upon comprehension of the *sense* of the harmony and good voice leading.

(d) Sight singing of examples in two to five parts. Use the figured chorales of Bach for two-part texture, a four-part chorale minus the tenor voice for three-part texture, and a four-voice chorale plus an additional voice composed by the instructor for five-voice texture. For example, sing the given chorale in the following ways:

(1) each voice separately;
(2) outer voices only, together;
(3) soprano, alto, and bass lines;
(4) all of the original four parts as set by Bach;
(5) all four plus the fifth voice added by the author.

Herr Christ der ein'ge Gott'ssohn.   J. S. Bach

XIII

Chords of Embellishment

We observed in an earlier chapter that certain structural harmonies may be embellished or ornamented by chords that are decorative and structurally unessential. In Volume I, Chapter XXI, this idea was mentioned in connection with the six-four chord, traditionally an unstable harmony. We noted there that this chord usually embellishes a more stable harmony in ways analogous to certain nonharmonic tones. Thus a passing six-four chord, although a complete chord, is analogous in function to a passing tone—chiefly because of the similarity in rhythmic and voice-leading factors. Of great importance in these chords of embellishment is the fact that the chord is understood not by virtue of its root but rather as a detail of linear or contrapuntal ornamentation.* Illustrations of embellishing chords that resemble nonharmonic tones in their decorative functions will be found in Examples I–IV below.

If the root of the chord does not explain adequately the function of the chord, we will call it a neighboring chord (N.C.), passing chord (P.C.), appoggiatura chord (App. C.), or the like, with the less important root analysis either in parenthesis or omitted altogether. This is particularly appropriate in the case of considerably altered chromatic harmonies, such as those in Examples I (*e*) and IV (*c*), where the roots seem coincidental, and where the chord members may be explained (1) as creating the sound of a familiar chord type (triad, dominant seventh, etc.) and (2) as the product of linear and melodic factors.

You will recall that when an appoggiatura occurs the harmony is analyzed in terms of the notes that will be present when the appoggiatura resolves. The same principle operates in connection with the appoggiatura chord, one of the most common forms of which is the V chord sounded above the root (or, occasionally, the third) of the I chord. This chord resolves into the complete I triad. It is particularly useful at cadences, where the penultimate V chord may be held over (in the manner of a suspension) while the bass (only) moves to the root of the I chord. Several examples of the V over I or $\frac{V}{I}$ are shown in Example III (see also Vol. II, Ch. XI, Ex. II(*e*)).

---

* See also Mitchell, Ch. 15, the section on pseudo-sevenths.

Example I. Evolution of the Passing Chord (P.C.).

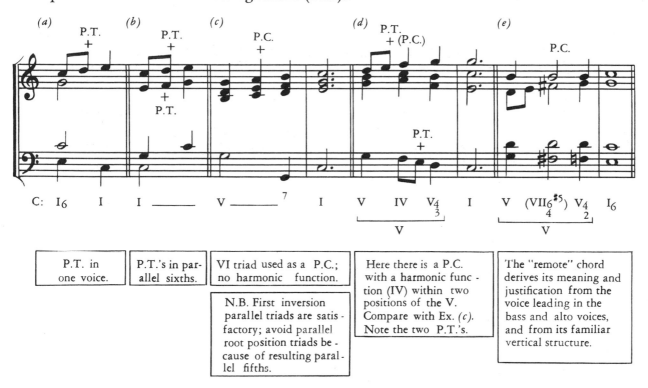

P.T. in one voice.	P.T.'s in parallel sixths.	VI triad used as a P.C.; no harmonic function.	Here there is a P.C. with a harmonic function (IV) within two positions of the V. Compare with Ex. *(c)*. Note the two P.T.'s.	The "remote" chord derives its meaning and justification from the voice leading in the bass and alto voices, and from its familiar vertical structure.

N.B. First inversion parallel triads are satisfactory; avoid parallel root position triads because of resulting parallel fifths.

Example II. Evolution of the Neighboring Chord (N.C.).

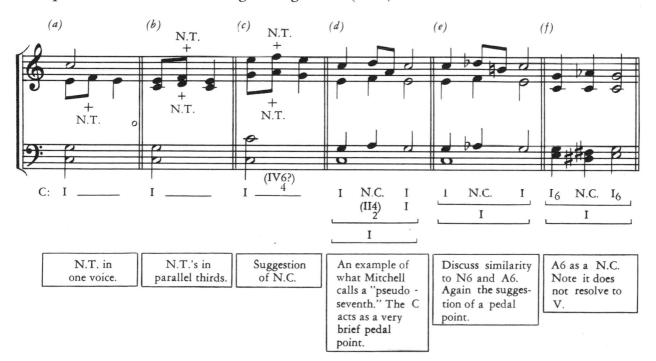

N.T. in one voice.	N.T.'s in parallel thirds.	Suggestion of N.C.	An example of what Mitchell calls a "pseudo-seventh." The C acts as a very brief pedal point.	Discuss similarity to N6 and A6. Again the suggestion of a pedal point.	A6 as a N.C. Note it does not resolve to V.

Example III. Appoggiaturas and Appoggiatura Chords (App. C.).

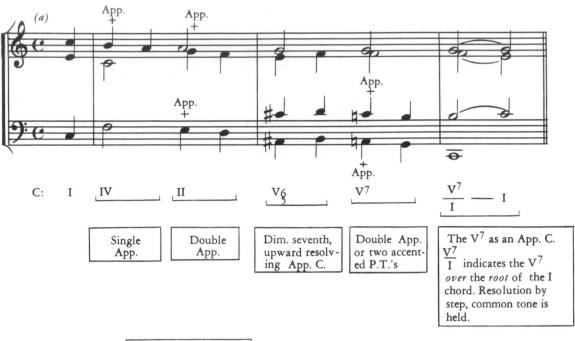

C: I   IV   II   V⅗   V⁷   V⁷/I — I

| Single App. | Double App. | Dim. seventh, upward resolving App. C. | Double App. or two accented P.T.'s | The V⁷ as an App. C. $\frac{V^7}{I}$ indicates the V⁷ *over* the *root* of the I chord. Resolution by step, common tone is held. |

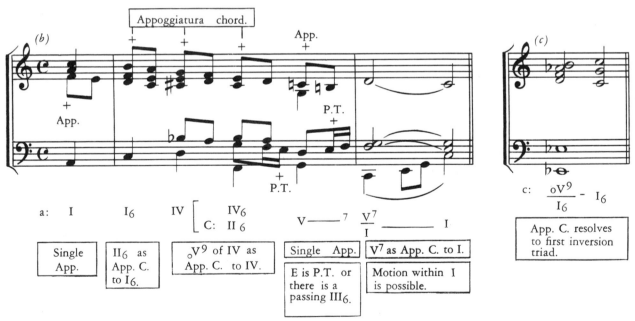

a: I   I₆   IV ⌈ IV₆ / C: II₆   V ——⁷ V⁷/I —— I

c: $\frac{oV^9}{I_6}$ - I₆

| Single App. | II₆ as App. C. to I₆. | oV⁹ of IV as App. C. to IV. | Single App. / E is P.T. or there is a passing III₆. | V⁷ as App. C. to I. / Motion within I is possible. |

App. C. resolves to first inversion triad.

Example IV. Other Types of Embellishing Chords.

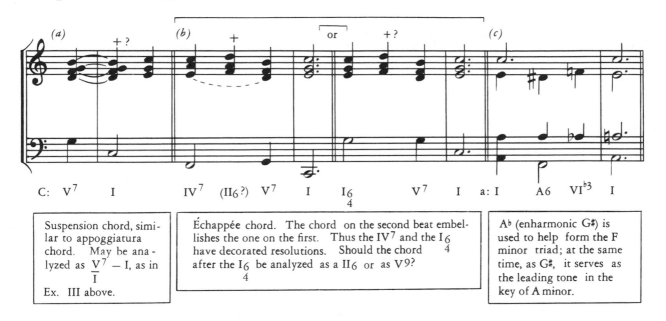

C: V⁷ I   IV⁷ (II₆?) V⁷ I I₆₄   V⁷ I   a: I   A6 VI^b3 I

Suspension chord, similar to appoggiatura chord. May be analyzed as $\frac{V^7}{I}$ — I, as in Ex. III above.	Échappée chord. The chord on the second beat embellishes the one on the first. Thus the IV⁷ and the I₆ have decorated resolutions. Should the chord after the I₆₄ be analyzed as a II₆ or as V⁹?	A♭ (enharmonic G♯) is used to help form the F minor triad; at the same time, as G♯, it serves as the leading tone in the key of A minor.

SUGGESTED EXERCISES

(a) Harmonize, using a passing chord at each asterisk. Analyze.

(b) Harmonize, using a neighboring chord at each asterisk. Analyze.

(c) Harmonize, using appoggiatura chords. Analyze.

(d) Using I VI IV N6 V I as the harmonic basis of each, write four phrases illustrating in turn

(1) passing chords,
(2) neighboring chords,
(3) appoggiatura chords,
(4) a mixture of several types.

(e) Sing the following melody. Then prepare a piano accompaniment using a few embellishing chords of several types in addition to the ones indicated.

XIV

Supplementary Exercises, Reading, and Discussion

Read the following and prepare for class discussion:

Sessions, Ch. 13. (Chordal ambiguity, the diminished seventh and the augmented triad, the enharmonic use of augmented sixth chords, etc.) See also the suggested exercises, page 368.

Piston, Ch. 25. (Other chromatic chords: the augmented fifth, the diminished fifth, appoggiatura chords, modulation.) Examine Piston's Examples 579 and 582. Analyze them. See also the exercises at the end of Ch. 25.

SUGGESTED EXERCISES

(a) Write in four-part harmony, and then improvise at the keyboard, one or more phrases involving modulations between the following keys. Use a few embellishing chords in the process. Include an appoggiatura chord at the final cadence.

    (1)   From A to f♯

    (2)   From g to E♭

    (3)   From D to e

    (4)   From c to B♭

(b) Improvise three different resolutions for each of the following diminished seventh chords. Explain each. In addition, indicate the spelling of at least two enharmonic equivalents for each chord, then resolve. Explain.

    (1)   d – f – a♭ – c♭

    (2)   e – g – b♭ d♭

    (3)   a – c – e♭ – g♭

(c) Play in several major keys:

    I I$^{\sharp 5}$ IV IV$^{\sharp 5}$ II V^9 I

(d) Improvise continuations of the following in several minor keys:

    (1) I IV ♯IV N6 . . . (establish N6 as tonic of new key).
            (= V$_2^4$ of
              N6)

    (2) I IV ♯IV N6 . . . (using N6 as IV of new key).

XV

Exercise in Composition

At least one week should be allowed to prepare a project, the specifications of which are to be determined by the instructor. The work should reflect familiarity with the materials of the course to date. The student should review the suggestions offered in Chapter X. Detailed analysis should accompany the finished product. If possible, the compositions should be performed by members of the class. The music should be not only "correct" but also imaginative and resourceful.

XVI

Ninth, Eleventh, and Thirteenth Chords

It is possible to superimpose additional thirds on the seventh chord in order to build ninth, eleventh, and thirteenth chords. In actual practice many of these so-called chords are really combinations of chord tones and nonharmonic tones, the latter usually distinguishable as appoggiaturas, suspensions, pedal points, passing or neighboring tones, échappées, and the like. When, through frequency of usage and familiarity of sound, these nonharmonic or "accessory" tones become "frozen" or indistinguishable from the true chord members, then a new chord is added to the harmonic vocabulary. New words in spoken language are created similarly by usage, and only later accredited by retrospective theory.

This principle simplified might be stated as follows: "Today's dissonances are tomorrow's consonances." There is considerable evidence to illustrate such a development in the early 17th century with respect to the seventh of the seventh chord, which was at first treated like a passing tone (on an unaccented beat) or as a suspension (if tied over to a strong from a weak beat). In many cases such a tone could be analyzed equally well as either a chord tone or a nonharmonic tone (see Ex. A in the Appendix, mm. 2, 6, 11, etc.).

Ninth Chords. Before studying nondominant ninth chords, the student should review dominant ninths in Chapter XI (see also Piston, Ch. 18, and Mitchell, Ch. 16).

In four-part harmony the fifth of the ninth chord is customarily omitted and the seventh is characteristically present. If the seventh were absent the ninth would be deprived of the "dissonant" seventh upon which it is constructed as an additional third, and the "ninth" might then be heard as a nonharmonic tone, or even as an "added second" (see Ch. XXVI).

Ninth chords are found most frequently in root position, occasionally in first, second, or third inversion, almost never in fourth inversion. It is generally wise to avoid more than two intervals of the second in immediate juxtaposition, otherwise the essentially tertial (third-based) nature of the harmony will disappear.

The chord-ninth, like the chord seventh, usually resolves down stepwise in the following chord, but there are occasional exceptions where the expected resolution appears transferred to a different voice—or it may be implicit in the harmony (or in the overtones of the root) but not explicitly sounded.

Example I. Transferred Resolution of the Chord-Ninth.

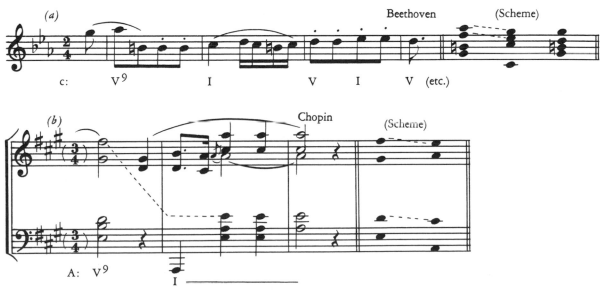

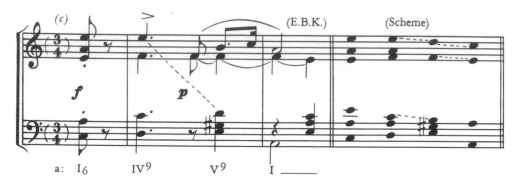

The chord of resolution is frequently a triad or a seventh chord, sometimes another ninth chord. If the chord-ninth is (1) unaccented, and resolves at once in the next chord, or (2) accented, and resolves within the same chord, then it might be preferable (because a simpler analysis) to call the apparent "ninth" a nonharmonic tone. In the event both the seventh and the ninth resolve within the chord, the analysis should probably indicate a double appoggiatura (or other nonharmonic tone). The rhythmic context of the chord-ninth and its resolution is thus very important in determining whether the ninth has either a structural or a purely decorative function.

Nondominant Ninth Chords. As indicated above, nondominant ninth chords appear in music less frequently than dominant ninth chords. The general principles stated above for all ninth chords should be considered equally valid for dominant and nondominant ninths. The customary absence of the fifth, inversion preferences, resolution principles, and so forth, are the same. The chief differences lie in the internal structure of the chords, demonstrated below:

(1) V^9 is built on V^7 (*dominant* seventh structure); for example, GBDF + A.

(2) I^9 and IV^9 are built on *major* seventh structures; for example, CEGB + D, and FACE + G.

(3) II^9, III^9, and VI^9 are built on *minor* seventh structures; for example, EGBD + F, and ACEG + B.

(4) The theoretical VII^9 or $_oV^{11}$ is not used, as a rule, because of the very harsh dissonance between the leading tone and the tonic which would be the inevitable result.

Example II. Nondominant Ninth Chords, and Similar Structures.

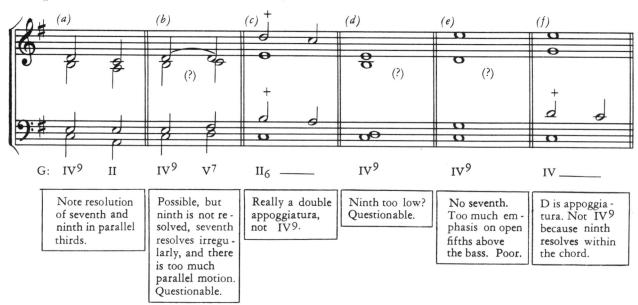

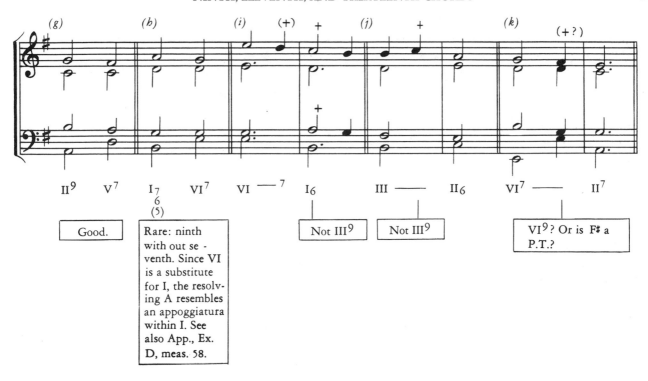

Example III. Sample Spacing of Ninth-Chord Inversions:*

Eleventh Chords. This is a comparatively uncommon chord. It almost always appears as a V^{11} in root position, and in open rather than closed position. The third of the chord does not sound well with the eleventh (a minor ninth away), so the third is customarily omitted. In four-part writing the ninth may be omitted also, leaving root, fifth, seventh, and eleventh. In a five-part chord only the third should be omitted. As in the case of the ninth, the accented eleventh should resolve in the next chord if it is a true chord tone. If it resolves within the harmony it should be analyzed as a nonharmonic tone. Curiously, all the examples cited in Piston are of the latter type (see his Ex. 463–9 and 471) and not true elevenths at all. (See assignment at the end of this chapter.)

---

* See Ch. XI for figuration of ninth-chord inversions.

Example IV. Eleventh Chords: Their Figuration and Usage.

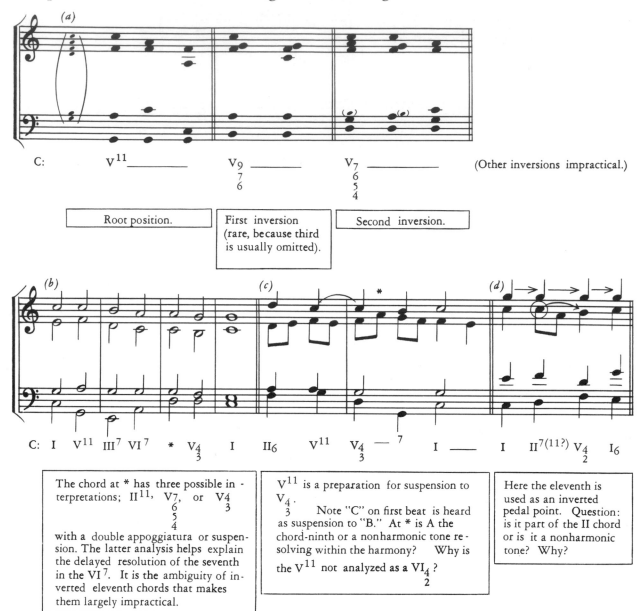

The chord at * has three possible interpretations; II^{11}, $V_7^{\ 6}_{\ 5}_{\ 4}$, or $V_{\ 3}^4$ with a double appoggiatura or suspension. The latter analysis helps explain the delayed resolution of the seventh in the VI^7. It is the ambiguity of inverted eleventh chords that makes them largely impractical.

V^{11} is a preparation for suspension to $V_{\ 3}^4$. Note "C" on first beat is heard as suspension to "B." At * is A the chord-ninth or a nonharmonic tone resolving within the harmony? Why is the V^{11} not analyzed as a $VI_{\ 2}^4$?

Here the eleventh is used as an inverted pedal point. Question: is it part of the II chord or is it a nonharmonic tone? Why?

II^{11} is rare. Note chromatic resolution in next chord, justified by the momentum of the ascending alto line.

Thirteenth Chords. This chord customarily appears only as a V^{13} and is generally in root position and open position. It may be regarded as an outgrowth of the V^7 decorated by an appoggiatura or échappée. In four-part writing the root, third, seventh, and thirteenth are used; the fifth, ninth, and eleventh are generally omitted. The chord-thirteenth appears most frequently in the soprano voice and resolves in the next chord in the following manner: either

(1) down stepwise, like an appoggiatura or seventh;

(2) up a third to the 5th scale degree, or (more likely) down a third to the tonic; or

(3) the tone may be held over, as a common tone in the following tonic chord, and not "resolved" in the customary sense at all.

Example V. Thirteenth Chords: Their Figuration and Usage.

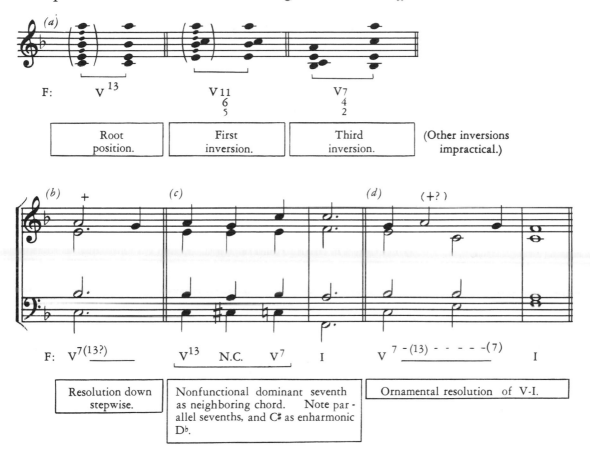

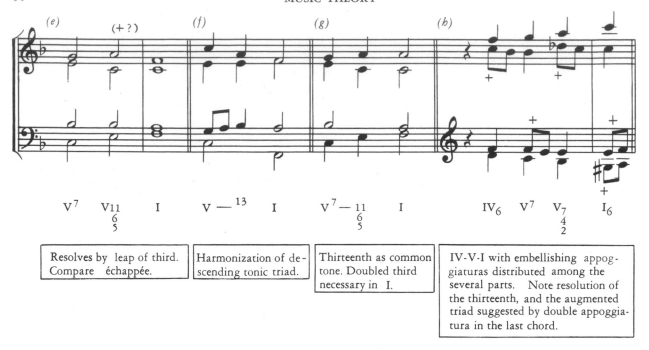

V⁷   V₁₁   I   V — ¹³   I   V⁷ — ¹¹   I   IV₆   V⁷   V₇   I₆
      ⁶   ⁶   ⁴
      ⁵   ⁵   ²

| Resolves by leap of third. Compare échappée. | Harmonization of descending tonic triad. | Thirteenth as common tone. Doubled third necessary in I. | IV-V-I with embellishing appoggiaturas distributed among the several parts. Note resolution of the thirteenth, and the augmented triad suggested by double appoggiatura in the last chord. |

SUGGESTED READING

Piston, Ch. 21.

————

SUGGESTED EXERCISES

(a) Write three one-measure examples in four-part harmony in the key of F major, illustrating the VI⁹ in root position and inverted, and two one-measure examples illustrating the "apparent" ninth as a justifiable nonharmonic tone. Resolve the chord-ninth down stepwise. End each example on I.

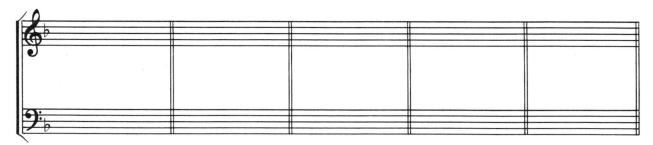

(b) List, in order, *your* analyses of the so-called eleventh chords in Piston, Ex. 463–9 and 471. Examine the "formulae" at the end of Chapter 21 in Piston, and write your own analyses in the light of the ideas set forth above.

(c) Write several one-measure examples in four-part harmony showing both structural and ornamental eleventh and thirteenth chords.

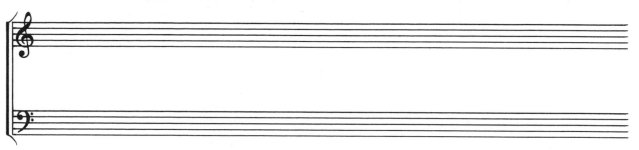

(d) Compose two short phrases using one or two examples each of the ninth, eleventh, and thirteenth chords.

(e) Play at the keyboard in several major and minor keys:

(1) I V^9 I

(2) I IV^9 II V^7 I

(3) I VI^9 V^7 V^9 I
       of V

(4) I V^{11} V^7 VI IV I
      of VI

(f) Play in the major mode only, in several keys:

I II_6 V^7 $V^{13}*$ I
   of III

(g) Play in the minor mode only, in several keys:

I N6 V^7 $V^{13}*$ I
   of III

(h) Sing, using syllables, then numbers. Discuss harmonization possibilities. Then harmonize at the piano.

---

* Deceptive resolution, V substituting for expected III.

XVII

Chromatically Altered Chords (Part Four)

The most frequently employed chromatically altered chords have been considered in Chapters III and VII. For further study and for illustrations of some of the less common altered chords, you are referred to the discussion and exercises in the Suggested Reading below.

Example I illustrates some of the many ways in which a single chord (here, the II chord in the minor mode) may be altered chromatically. In (*a*) we have a Neapolitan sixth chord (already an altered II chord) further altered by having its third lowered. In measure two the E♭ in the tenor (chord-seventh) is resolved in the alto after having been transferred to that voice.

In (*b*) the B♮ is employed to avoid the augmented second; the cross relation with B♭ is permitted. The ♯5 changes the diminished triad to a minor one.

The II⁷ in example (*c*) has been changed from a half-diminished seventh chord to an augmented sixth chord by virtue of the ♯3. Note well the leap out of the chord-seventh (D), and the understood progression D-D♯.

The third chord in (*d*) sounds not only strange but rather unlike any recognizable chord structure. The apparent sixth in the lower voices sounds like a perfect fifth. An unexplainable chord such as this should not be used.

Example (*e*) employs three different alterations of II. Note the deceptive resolution of the V⁷ of IV; could this chord also be analyzed as an altered IV⁷ of V? Observe further the enharmonic change C-B♯ in the soprano. The entire progression is a large II-V.

Example I. Alterations of the II Chord.

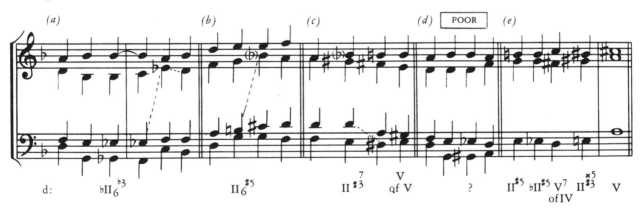

SUGGESTED READING

Sessions, Ch. 12, parts 3 and 4 (pp. 339–46).

SUGGESTED EXERCISES

(a) Prepare a harmonic analysis of the Brahms Intermezzo, opus 76, no. 7.* The analysis should include a study of chords and chord groups, phrase structure and cadences, nonharmonic tones, tonicization and modulation, etc.

---

* See the list of Suggested Supplementary Materials, p. vii.

(b) Write several examples showing various alterations of the IV chord (in the major or minor mode). Use Example I as an illustration of procedure. Explain or justify each alteration. Watch the voice leading carefully. Analyze thoroughly.

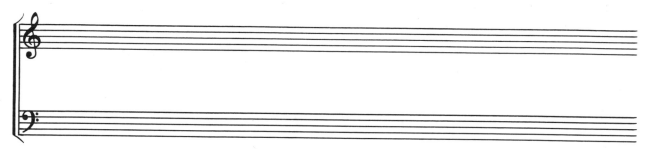

(c) Using Example I as a guide, play I VI II V I in six versions, each with a different set of alterations. For example:

(1)   I   ♭VI   N6   V♭5   I   (in the major mode),

(2)   I   ♯VI⁷   V⁷   V   I   (in the minor mode),
                of V

and so forth.

XVIII

Modulation (Part Two)

In addition to the pivotal diatonic common chord discussed in Chapter I (Vol. II), there are several other means, devices, or mechanisms which may be employed in effecting a change of key. Although less frequently used they are equally important, and of course necessary if there is to be a modulation to a key that does not have any chord in common. Some of them are listed below:

(1) Modulation using secondary dominant, Picardy third, or Neapolitan sixth as a common chord. These chords appear so commonly within the key that they may be used without any sense of strangeness in effecting a modulation. Although not in the diatonic scale, they may operate in a fashion similar to the diatonic chords in common chord modulation. The altered chord in one key is generally a diatonic (unaltered) chord in the other key (see Ex. I).

(2) Chromatic alteration. Chromatic change of one or more chord tones may be used in modulating. It is perhaps better (smoother) to alter only one tone, if possible, so the others may be common to both keys. These common tones help to provide continuity, and in a sense perform the same function as a common chord: they provide the pivot, hinge, or connection between the two keys (see Ex. II).

(3) Enharmonic change. This device is useful in modulating to a remote tonality, particularly from a flat key to a sharp key (or vice versa). A *single* chord may be subject to analysis both in the sharp and in the flat key. The augmented sixth chord, for example, may be the enharmonic equivalent of a V^7 in another key. Occasionally *two* chords are involved, suggesting a parallel with the chromatic alteration type discussed above (see Ex. III).

(4) Modulating sequence. The sequence* may include a series of real or only apparent modulations. The development section of a sonata or symphony movement not uncommonly employs the modulating sequence in order to secure the sense of temporary tonal instability that is desired as a contrast to the more stable exposition and recapitulation sections. Firm establishment of the new key at the close of the modulating sequence is desirable, otherwise the musical ear will project an indefinite continuation of the modulatory procedure. The logical compulsion of the sequence is similar to the idea of inertia in physics, i.e. there is a tendency for matter in motion to continue moving in the same direction unless affected by an outside force. In music this outside force is a new idea (such as a cadential formula) following the sequence (see Ex. IV).

(5) A single tone. One note alone may be used as a pivot, as the only common element in making a modulation. Sometimes this single tone remains after the chord as such has ceased sounding, and the unharmonized tone may be a common tone in the new key. Or the unharmonized single tone may move (frequently by a half-step) to another (perhaps unharmonized) tone in a new key. Beethoven uses this device frequently (see the transition between the second and third movements of his Piano Concerto no. 5). So does Schubert, whose modulations still seem bold and daring a century later. This type of modulation is effective between large sections and divisions, but not in the course of a phrase or short structural unit (see Ex. V).

Examples I–V below illustrate the means discussed in the paragraphs above.

---

* See Vol. I, Ch. XXVII.

Example I. Familiar Altered Chord Type as "Common Chord."

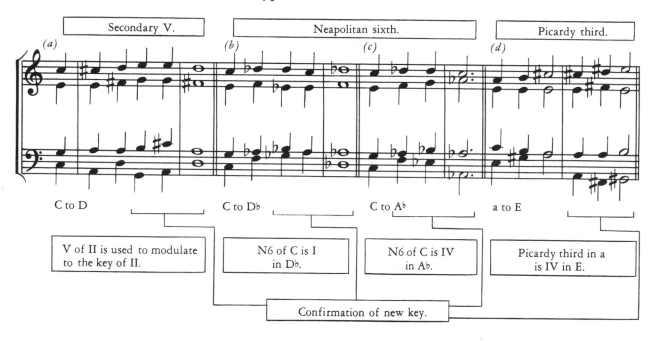

Example II. Chromatic Alteration.

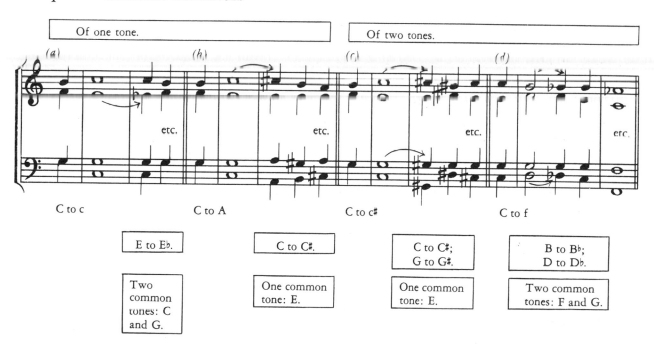

Example III. Enharmonic Change.

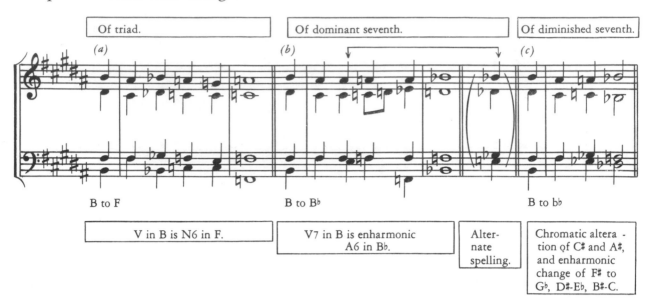

Example IV. Modulating Sequence.

The sequence above modulates from D minor to D♭ major. Note the difference between the chord groups and the key groups. Questions on the above (question pertains to chord above similar number):

(1) Why is there a B♮ in the bass rather than a B♭?

(2) How can one justify the deceptive resolution of the augmented sixth chord?

(3) Why A♯ rather than B♭?

(4) Explain the derivation and function of the A6 here.

(5) What happens to the sequence at this point, and at (6)?

Locate all the chromatic passing tones and discuss the ornamented cadence.

Example V. Modulation by One Tone (in this Example, C).

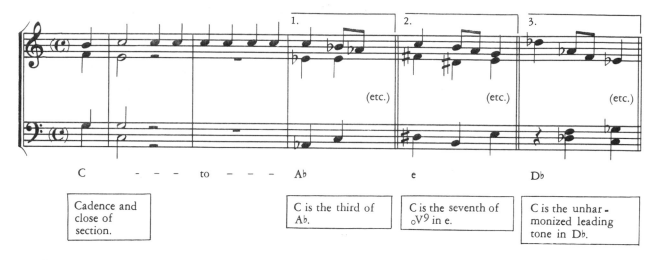

C　－　－　－　to　－　－　－　Ab　　　　　e　　　　　Db

| Cadence and close of section. | C is the third of Ab. | C is the seventh of $_{o}V^{9}$ in e. | C is the unhar-monized leading tone in Db. |

Suggested Reading

Sessions, Ch. 11, 13 (sect. 1–3), and the exercises on pp. 372 and 380.
Piston, Ch. 19 (sections on the modulating sequence). See also his Ex. 419–21 and Ex. e, on p. 223.

SUGGESTED EXERCISES

(a) Write three to four measure phrases in $\frac{3}{4}$ or $\frac{4}{4}$, modulating as follows:

    (1) from D major to F♯ major, using G as N6;
    (2) from D major to F♯ minor, using E as V of III in F♯ minor;
    (3) from D minor to F♯ minor, using Picardy third in D minor;
    (4) from E♭ major to F major, altering E♭ chromatically;
    (5) from E♭ major to C minor, chromatically altering the V in E♭;
    (6) from E♭ major to C♯ minor, using enharmonic equivalents as a pivot;
    (7) from A major to A♭ major, in a modulating sequence.

(b) Practice transposing the above exercises at the keyboard up a perfect fourth, up a perfect fifth, and so forth.

(c) Using Brahms's *Works for the Piano,* Vol. II,* describe the modulatory procedures and devices employed at the following points:

    (1) op. 76, no. 2, mm. 11–13 (the second ending), and mm. 44–6 (at the double bar);
    (2) op. 79, no. 1, at each of the six changes of key signature;
    (3) op. 79, no. 2, at both changes of key signature;
    (4) op. 116, no. 6, at both changes of key signature;
    (5) op. 118, no. 3, at both changes of key signature;
    (6) op. 119, no. 3, measures 12–13 and 28–9.

---

* See the list of Suggested Supplementary Materials, p. vii.

(d) Sing several modulating melodies. Use numbers or syllables. Examine each melody first to determine where the modulation takes place. Put an asterisk or star at the point of modulation. Then, when singing the melody, change number or syllable system at the appropriate place. For example:

a: 1   4   3   2   1   2   7   5   5   7   2   4   3   (etc. in d. Mark the next modulations.)

(e) Dictation of unaccompanied modulating melodies and modulating phrases in three- and four-part harmony. The modulations should be of the type discussed in this chapter.

XIX

The Relationship of Harmony to Larger Formal Units

In the music of the common-practice period (roughly 1700–1890), form is to a large extent a product of harmonic organization. This statement is not intended to minimize the importance of other musical elements such as thematic materials which, when contrasted, varied, or repeated, provide additional means of securing musical form.

A large musical composition has many of the same elements as a phrase, a period, or a small form—except that these elements are now much more extended. For example, a single four-measure phrase might be an expansion of the simple formula I to V, V back to I. This might be equally possible in a period in which the first phrase ended on V, the second on I. Or it might be found in a complete movement in binary form, like so many of the Scarlatti sonatas, where the progression I to V may be extended to two pages. Viewed in this light, the V chord which provides a half-cadence, the V chord tonicized (so it sounds *almost* like I), and the key of the dominant would differ in *degree* rather than in *kind*. The term "V" is relative rather than absolute, and its meaning is determined by the *level of analysis*.

Taking into account these principles together with what is already understood about phrase-period structure, prepare a diagrammatic analysis of the form of Brahms's Intermezzo, op. 76, no. 7, complete.

Your diagram should show, for example, the elaborate prolongation of the III chord in A minor in the middle of the first phrase (the foreshadowing of a still greater emphasis on III), which on a different level might be conceived as a modulation to C major. To show these different levels, use a schematic diagram similar to the one in Example I below.

Show the levels as follows:

(1) Your lowest (most fundamental) level should show only the major divisions of the piece (the modulatory scheme) in terms of the prevailing tonality. Use Roman numerals to indicate modulations; thus a first section in the tonic, a second in the key of the dominant, and a third in the tonic would be shown as C:I-V-I, *not* C:I, G:I, C:I.

(2) The next higher level would show the principal harmonic motions within each division. A cadential progression in the above-mentioned second section would be indicated, for example, as IV - I$_4^6$ - V - I in G, and *not* as C: I - V$_4^6$ - V of V - V.

(3) The next higher would show perhaps the basic harmony of each measure (if it can be reduced to one or two chords), or perhaps for two-measure groups.

(4) The highest level would show each chord in the literal sense.

Example I below is an analysis of part I of Brahms's Intermezzo, op. 117, no. 1, showing the interrelated, four-measure phrases. Roman numerals indicate harmonic structure. Arabic numerals show length in measures.

Example I. Diagram of Brahms's Intermezzo, Op. 117, No. 1, Measures 1-16.

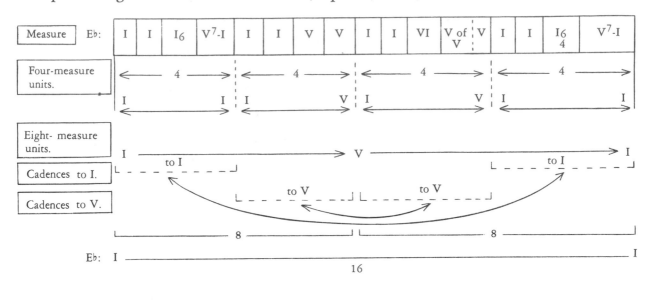

SUGGESTED EXERCISES

(a) Sing the following melody, using numbers, then syllables. Write a harmonization in free keyboard style. Then improvise an accompaniment at the keyboard.

(b) Sing the following melody as above. Harmonize in three parts, using a running eighth-note figure in the middle voice and a soprano line with contrasting rhythm and shape. (This might be scored for such instrumentation as is available in the class, and performed.) Improvise a keyboard harmonization, changing chords where there are repeated tones; keep the texture active where the bass is static and employ, in this connection, a few embellishing chords.

(c) Write 16 measures of music using the above diagram of Brahms's Intermezzo, op. 117, no. 1, as a structural outline. Do not employ Brahms's melody or accompaniment texture.

(d) Discuss the form of the above Brahms excerpt. In what way does it resemble a period? How does it differ?

(e) Rhythm drills.

XX

Exercise in Composition

Write a short composition, using the given melody. You may write in three- or four-voice texture, or freely in idiomatic piano style as you prefer. Your harmonic vocabulary should reflect familiarity with altered chords, and there should be a judicious use of nonharmonic tones. Be careful to make your modulations convincing by establishing the key unequivocally. Examine the cadences to be sure the feeling of rest this term implies is present. Observe the points of rest indicated by the commas. Label all nonharmonic tones in the customary fashion. Make a reduction to show the broad underlying harmonic structure.

XXI

Modal Harmony

At the opening of the contemporary era there were several stylistic trends, one of which may be regarded as a reaction against the ever-increasing complexity of harmonic vocabulary and the excesses of chromaticism that characterized some late 19th century music. This counter-trend favored not only the simpler forms of harmony (the triad) and diatonic scales, but also a return to the principles of part-writing and the medieval (ecclesiastical) modes employed during the pretonal renaissance and early baroque periods. (In the 1920's this trend developed further into the "white-note" school, and what Nicolas Slonimsky refers to as "pandiatonicism."*) This rather anti-chromatic music cannot be analyzed properly by the root-progression theory associated historically with the major-minor system of the 18th and 19th centuries. Curiously, composers using the chromatic style (which developed even greater complexities alongside this neomodal school) also began to find root-progression theory inadequate (as we shall see in subsequent chapters), and eventually, in Schoenberg's revolutionary twelve-tone theory, chords, roots, and tonality in the traditional sense of those terms are all rejected.

Some of the cardinal principles of modal harmony may be summarized as follows:

(1) Simple chord forms preferred (major or minor triads, familiar sevenths).

(2) Medieval modes preferred over major-minor modes.

(3) The leading tone† and the dominant function are eschewed, especially at cadences, chiefly in order to avoid the characteristic dynamic elements of the major-minor system, but partly in order to be freed from the undesired expectations and limitations that these elements inevitably create.

(4) Chord connections are not explained by the principle of root progression, but rather in terms of voice leading principles that are valid in both tonal and pretonal music, namely:

  (a) stepwise progression preferred;
  (b) common-tone connections where possible;
  (c) recognition of the bass as harmonic generator, and of the three basic types of bass progression (the step, the third, the perfect fourth or fifth);
  (d) sevenths characteristically resolve down stepwise in the next chord.

(5) Dissonance plays a comparatively lesser role in most neomodal music since the emphasis is on harmonic simplicity, but any of the familiar nonharmonic tones may be employed, and they resolve as in tonal music.

(6) Chromatic alterations should be used very sparingly to avoid disturbing the diatonic purity of the mode. Occasional chromaticism to suggest mixed modes, or a modulation, is of course possible. Chromatic half-steps and similar practices suggesting chromatic, major, or minor scale structure should be avoided in this style.

---

* See article on "Pandiatonicism" in *Grove's Dictionary of Music and Musicians,* 5th ed.

† The leading-tone principle, although absent from the ecclesiastical modes in their pure form, does appear in pretonal (modal) polyphonic music when the seventh degree is chromatically raised at melodic cadences to provide the intuitively desired half-step. This sense of "tonal magnetism" is more fully realized in the dynamic tonal organization of the later major-minor system.

Problems in Analysis. Analyze the following examples in terms of the criteria listed above. Instead of root analysis, consider the vertical structures as triads or, if sevenths, indicate what *type* of seventh they are. Use the following abbreviations:

TRIADS: T (major triad)

t (minor triad)

T₆ [t₆] (major [minor] triad in first inversion)

T₆⁄₄ [t₆⁄₄] (major [minor] triad in second inversion)

(No numerical indication is needed for root position. Diminished and augmented chords are not used, except for the diminished first inversion triad, O₆.)

SEVENTHS: The structural types of seventh chord are illustrated in Volume I, Chapter XXVI. Those marked below with an asterisk (*) are to be used sparingly because of their traditional, functional associations in tonal music.

D7* (dominant seventh)

O7 (diminished seventh)

Ø7 (half-diminished seventh)

M7 (major seventh)

m7 (minor seventh)

s7 (small seventh)

L7 (large seventh)

A6* (augmented sixth)

(Use the customary figured bass indications to show any inversions; thus D7 inversions are D₆⁄₅, D₄⁄₃, and D₄⁄₂.)

Example I.

Example II.

Example III.

SUGGESTED EXERCISES

(a) Write three modal melodies (unharmonized), eight to ten measures long. Two of them should be vocal in style and range, the third for a specific single-line instrument. At least one of the three should be in a transposed mode. The original (untransposed) modes are listed in Volume 1, Chapter II, Example II; and in Example III you will find each of these transposed so that the tonic (or final) note is C. The ecclesiastical modes, like the major and minor modes, may be transposed to any key. Begin your melody on the 1st, 3rd, or 5th scale degree. End on 1.

(b) Reharmonize the modal melodies in Examples I and II above. Use four-part harmony in one example and a free piano style in the other. (Alternate suggestion: reharmonize Ex. I, using the texture and style of Ex. II, and vice versa.) Limit the chords to those indicated in the above list.

(c) Harmonize at the keyboard ascending scales in the Dorian, Phrygian, Lydian, and Mixolydian modes. Use a bass line that is generally in contrary motion. (Note to the instructor: discuss at this time the "Phrygian cadence.")

(d) Sight singing of modal melodies:
   (1) composed by members of the class,
   (2) of the medieval and renaissance periods,
   (3) of the late 19th and early 20th centuries.

(e) Dictation of modal melodies and modal harmonizations.

(f) Write a short paper (200–300 words) in which you compare the principles of modal harmony with those of functional, root-related, tonal harmony.

XXII

Exercises in Analysis and Composition

(1) Study carefully the harmonic vocabulary and style, nonharmonic tone usage, phrase structure, and cadential formulas of :

    (a) two or three 16th-century works to be chosen by the instructor;

    (b) the modal harmonizations by Rimsky-Korsakoff of the three traditional Russian folksongs which follow (the texts have been omitted).

(2) One of the three modal melodies you composed last week should be selected by your instructor. Use this as a basis for a composition using modal harmony consistent with the stylistic principles found in the illustrations analyzed and discussed in class. The work may be for piano, voice and piano, or such instrumentation as will lend itself to performance by members of the class.

SUPPLEMENTARY EXERCISES

(a) Prepare at the keyboard modal harmonizations of :

    (1) a short melody to be supplied by the instructor;

    (2) one of the better student melodies composed for the assignment in the previous chapter;

or

    (3) one of the given Russian folksongs.

(b) Dictation of modal melodies and harmonizations.

(c) Continue sight singing the modal melodies composed for the assignment in the previous chapter. These may be written at the blackboard before the class meets, or run off on a multiple-copy machine.

Example I. "From the Forest Green" by Rimsky-Korsakoff. (Dorian Mode)

Example II. "The Mist Through the Valley Sweeping" by Rimsky-Korsakoff. (Mixolydian Mode)

Example III. "There is a Meadow" by Rimsky-Korsakoff. (Aeolian Mode)

XXIII

Chromatic Harmony

With this chapter we enter a new phase in the study of chromaticism. Let us review, briefly and in outline form, the several levels of chromatic alteration in the order we have studied them (which is from the simple to the complex):

(1) Alteration within the diatonic mode. This may be seen in the raised and lowered 6th and 7th degrees of the minor mode. The leading tone, it should be remembered, though altered from the key signature, is regarded as essential and proper to the minor mode except in the case of the III chord (where the lowered 7 is used to avoid the augmented triad), or where the descending form of the melodic minor mode leads 7 through 6 to 5.

(2) Modal alteration. If the 3rd scale degree is altered there is an unmistakable change of mode feeling. This may be observed in the Picardy third, where the 3rd is raised from minor to major (see Vol. II, Ch. VII). Since 6 and 7 in the melodic minor ascending form correspond to 6 and 7 in the major mode there is an ambiguity in the upper tetrachord. The 3rd scale degree (in the lower tetrachord) is most important, therefore, in establishing modal change.

(3) Chromatically altered nonharmonic tones (see Vol. II, Ch. II).

(4) Chromatically altered chords having a

    (a) dominant function (secondary dominant) (see Vol. II, Ch. III);

    (b) subdominant function (secondary II or IV, the Neapolitan sixth chord, augmented sixth chords) (see Vol. II, Ch. III and VII).

(5) Chromatically altered chords that are embellishing or decorative in nature, within an essentially diatonic framework (see Ch. XIII). In this category we find that the passing, neighboring, and similar functions usually associated with single tones (P.T., N.T., etc.) or with diatonic chords (passing, neighboring, or appoggiatura-like cadential six-four chord) can be assigned further to chords that are quite remote from the key. These chords, unlike those in category (4) above, have little harmonic function, and are really closer to category (3) since they are decorative. The chromaticism and the chords employed, then, are justified chiefly by melodic and voice-leading considerations. The root of such an embellishing chord thus is rather coincidental and nonfunctional (see the discussion of "pseudo-sevenths" in Mitchell, Ch. 15).

In Volume II, Chapter XIII (*Chords of Embellishment*), we saw that diatonic chords may be embellished by single chromatic chords. If one assumes that a group of such chromatic chords may be used in similar fashion (just as one may have three consecutive passing tones before resolution) then it follows that the chromatic element could assume an important role in the unfolding of the musical ideas, and almost overshadow the diatonic underpinning. As illustrations see the following quotations:

    Example I (excerpt from Franck's Symphony in D minor).
    Example II (excerpt from Bach's "Chromatic Fantasy and Fugue").
    Example III (excerpt from Wagner's opera "Tannhäuser").
    Example IV (the "Sleep" motive from Wagner's "The Ring of the Nibelung").
    Examples V and VI (two excerpts from Franck's "Prelude, Chorale, and Fugue").

Examples II and IV show the principle of the *circular extension*—similar to a complete circle of fifths—since at the close of the progression we have returned to the harmonic starting point. Such a chord group should be regarded as the embellishment of a single chord that appears, frame-like, as a structural support at the beginning and at the end.

Examples I, III, and V illustrate the embellishment by chromatic means of a phrase that is essentially a *progression* from I to V. In Example VI we see a modulation to the dominant minor by way of the supertonic in a *sequence* of chromatic chords.

In analyzing chromatic music one should distinguish between (1) the *structurally* important chords (whose roots are usually related to each other according to the established principles of diatonic harmony) and (2) the *embellishing* chords (whose roots may not seem conventionally related to each other or to the structural chords). These embellishing chords should be explained in terms of two factors:

(a) the voice leading, or chord connection (either (1) a stepwise progression—preferably a half-step—or (2) a common tone—which may be an enharmonic equivalent—in the same register or in another register);

(b) the chord type (usually a triad or one of the following types of seventh chords):

   (1) dominant seventh chord (D7),

   (2) diminished seventh chord (O7),

   (3) half-diminished seventh chord ($\emptyset$7),

   (4) augmented sixth chord (A6).

Nonharmonic tones appear perhaps less frequently here than in diatonic music, since the need for dissonant embellishment is not as great. The nonharmonic tones that are employed will sometimes be used in such a manner that the notes in question could be analyzed equally and as satisfactorily as chord tones: the distinction between chord tone and nonharmonic tone begins to disappear (see Ex. VII for an elaboration of this idea). The gradual disappearance of dissonance in the development of chromatic music is consummated in the music of Schoenberg and his followers, for twelve-tone theory (upon which most of this music is based) denies the existence of dissonance, the protests of some listeners to the contrary notwithstanding!

Example I. An Illustration of Procedure in Analyzing Chromatic Music: Excerpt from Franck's Symphony in D Minor.

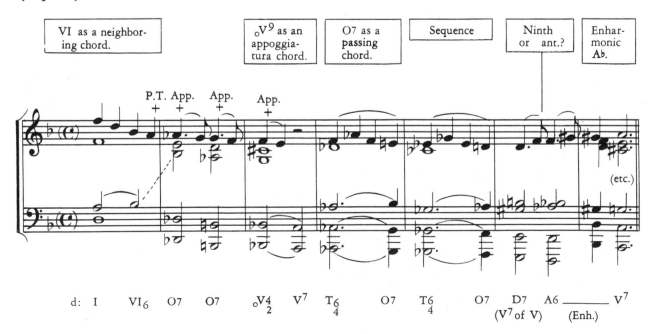

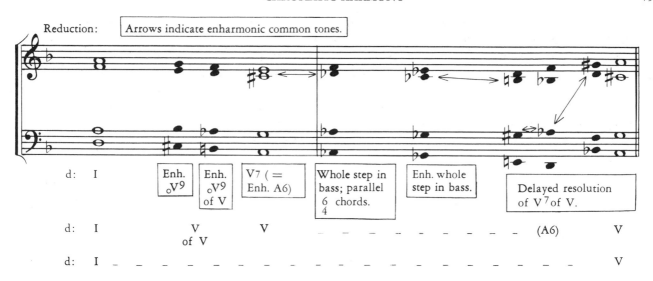

Reduction: | Arrows indicate enharmonic common tones. |

| d: I | Enh. ₀V⁹ | Enh. ₀V⁹ of V | V7 (= Enh. A6) | Whole step in bass; parallel 6/4 chords. | Enh. whole step in bass. | Delayed resolution of V⁷ of V. |

d: I   V   V
              of V

(A6)   V

d: I _ _ _ _ _ _ _ _ _ _ _ _ _ _ _ _ _ V

(See Ch. XXI for explanation of symbols T, O7, D7, etc.)

Example II. Excerpt from Bach's "Chromatic Fantasy and Fugue."

d: I

(etc.)

₀V⁹ _____ I
I

Reduction:

Example III. Excerpt from Wagner's Opera "Tannhäuser."

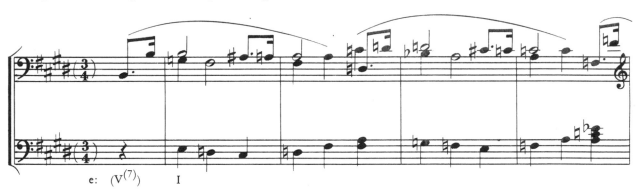

Reduction:

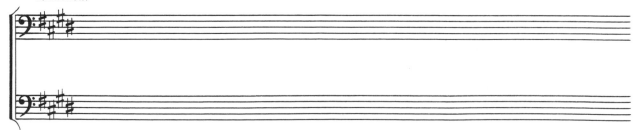

Example IV. The "Sleep" Motive from Wagner's "The Ring of the Nibelung."

E: I   I

Reduction:

Example V. Excerpt (♯1) from Franck's "Prelude, Chorale, and Fugue."

Eb: I

V
(Bb: I)

Reduction:

Example VI. Excerpt (♯2) from Franck's "Prelude, Chorale, and Fugue."

Example VII. The Ambiguous Use of Chord Tones as Nonharmonic Tones.

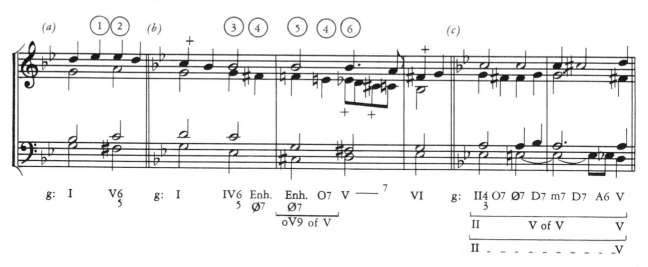

Questions: (see numbers above staff)

(1) N.T. or root of VI?

(2) Appoggiatura or seventh of F♯⁷ chord?

(3) Appoggiatura or fifth of C⁷ chord?

(4) P.T. or part of seventh chord? Resolution of appoggiatura?

(5) Appoggiatura or seventh of enharmonic G⁷ chord (∅7)?

(6) Appoggiatura or root of augmented VI triad?

SUGGESTED EXERCISES

(a) Analyze Examples II–VI carefully and thoroughly, following the model provided (excerpt from the first movement of Franck's Symphony in D minor). Procedure: (1) Analyze structurally significant chords in terms of their roots, and relate them in chord groups. (2) Embellishing chords should be analyzed primarily as triads or seventh chords without regard for root, and only secondarily in conventional root-progression terminology. (3) Note carefully all voice leading connections and implications. (4) Make a reduction showing the structural chords in whole notes and the embellishing chords in solid note heads (as in the model), keeping the soprano and bass lines as close to the original as possible.

(b) Improvise at the keyboard a harmonization in chromatic style based upon the following scheme:

> melody line: 8 7 ♭7 6 ♭6 5
> root progression: I V
>   (passing   (half
>   chords) cadence)

(c) Sing the following melodies. Then improvise an appropriate keyboard harmonization.

(d) Sight singing of chromatic melodies within a given key.

(e) Dictation of chromatic melodies and harmonic progressions.

XXIV

Exercises in Analysis

Analyze the following, all in Volume II of *Works for the Piano* by Johannes Brahms:*

(1) Rhapsody, opus 79, no. 2, measures 1–13.

Make a schematic reduction of these measures. Show the sequential patterns in measures 1–8 and the "return" to G minor in measure 11. Note the apparent conflict between the *bass* progressions and the *root* progressions over the bar line into measures 1 and 5. Observe in measure 4 the "double meaning" of G major (a) as parallel major of G minor, and (b) as VI in B minor. The parallel major of B minor (B major) becomes V of E minor in measure 8; but the E minor in turn becomes VI of G major which then changes to G minor. This may be viewed in the long run as motion within G minor, or in closer view as a mirror-like, somewhat circular modulatory pattern (g-G-b-B-e-G-g) with an emphasis on parallel (major-minor) relationships and third-related keys. The cadence at measure 13 helps to prepare the key of the next section, D minor (the minor dominant of the prevailing key of G minor).

(2) Intermezzo, opus 119, no. 1, measures 1–5 (first beat).

Make a schematic reduction of these measures. Show how the apparent ninth or eleventh chords may be more clearly interpreted as part of the following progression:

$$\boxed{\text{b:}} \quad \text{I} \quad \text{IV}^9 \quad \text{V}^7 \quad \text{III} \quad \text{III}^7 \quad \text{VI} \quad \underset{\text{of III}}{\quad} \text{II}^7 \quad \text{I}_6 \; \text{V}_4 \; \text{I}_6$$
$$ \underset{42}{}$$

$$\boxed{\text{roots:}} \quad \text{b} - \text{e} \; - \text{a} - \text{d} \quad - \quad \text{g} \; - \text{c}\sharp - \text{f}\sharp - \text{b}$$

N.B. The root progression creates a complete circle of fifths in B minor.

(3) Intermezzo, opus 118, no. 1, measures 1–10.

The rather ambiguous tonality of the opening measures is complex and not easy to explain. Since the work ends in the key of A minor (on I$^{\sharp 3}$) it would seem proper to analyze the beginning in A minor, with a modulation to C major at the first double bar, rather than analyze the music at once in C (the key at the first cadence) or in F (suggested by the B♮ in measure 1). Make a schematic reduction of measures 1–10 showing the following chords in root-progression analysis:

$$\text{a}_6 \quad \text{F}_6 \quad \text{Aug. 6} \quad \text{D}^7 \quad \text{G}^9 \quad \frac{\text{G}^7}{\text{C}} \; - \quad \text{C}$$

Show a common chord modulation from A minor to C major. Show also the possible analyses VI, IV, II, V, I in C major; and I, VI, II of III (V of V of III), V of III, III in A minor. What evidence of F major is there in addition to the B♮ in measure 1?

(4) Ballade, opus 118, no. 3, measures 1–23.

The opening period consists of two five-measure phrases (an antecedent and a consequent). The antecedent comes to a half-close (semi-cadence) on V; the consequent, which begins with parallel materials, veers off into a modified sequential relationship to the antecedent, and closes on a Picardy third (I$^{\sharp 3}$) in G minor (*not* I in G major) and a perfect authentic cadence somewhat weakened by the continuing accompaniment motion and the introduction of the chord-seventh on the third quarter of the measure. Explain the modulation procedure in measures 10 and 21.

---

* See list of Suggested Supplementary Materials, p. vii.

(5) Capriccio, opus 116, no. 7, measures 1-2.

Show how the four chords of these two measures can be related by fifths with respect to their roots if the principle of the secondary dominant is employed.

(6) Intermezzo, opus 116, no. 6, measures 1–24.

This is perhaps the most chromatic example among Brahms's piano works, and illustrates some of the points made in the last chapter.

    (a) Explain the second chord. Is B♮ or B♯ a nonharmonic tone?

    (b) What is the harmonic implication of the bass line in the first phrase (the first two measures)?

    (c) Is the B♯ in measure 3 analogous to the B♯ in measure 1? Explain.

    (d) What is the main harmonic progression from the opening chord to measure 4, beat 2?

    (e) Are measures 5-6 analogous to 1-2? If so, explain the F♯ minor key feeling. Is there a modulation here (if so, where is it confirmed, or why) or is F♯ only II in E?

    (f) What kind of a cadence in what key do you find in measure 8? Give your reasons.

    (g) Explain the oddly spelled chords in measures 12-13-14. In what key will you analyze them and why?

    (h) At measure 15 is the music analogous to the beginning? Explain.

    (i) Name the basic structural chords in the chromatic passage from measures 18–24. Compare the procedure here with that illustrated in Example VII, Chapter XXIII. Which chords are obviously embellishments of other chords? Which chords are absolutely necessary in going from the tonicized F♯ (meas. 18) to E (meas. 22)?

    (j) Explain the G♯ minor six-four chord in measures 23-24.

SUPPLEMENTARY EXERCISES

(a) Sing the following melody, using syllables, numbers, or a neutral vowel sound.

Adagio ed espressivo

(b) Compose a written harmonization of the melody above in a free piano style or for such instrumentation as may be available among the students. The product should be played in class. The instructor may wish to invite discussion regarding the merits of the compositions performed.

(c) Improvise an accompaniment at the keyboard, using the melody of Exercise (a) above. Watch the voice leading, try to use more half- than whole-steps, and look for possible common chord tones. There should be occasional well-defined cadences with structurally related harmonies. Limit your chords to those suggested in previous chapters, and chiefly to the ones listed in Chapter XXIII.

(d) Practice modulating from any given key to another whose distance is a tritone, using chromatically related triads and seventh chords of the type suggested in Chapter XXIII. The final chord should be I in the new key, and it should be reached smoothly, naturally, and with emphasis on stepwise progression (preferably half-steps) and common tones. Suggested procedure: have outer voices proceed by half-steps in contrary motion.

(e) Dictation of chromatic harmonic progressions and melodies.

(f) Further sight singing of chromatic melodies. Suggested sources: works by Franck, Wagner, Bruckner, Wolf, Liszt.

XXV

Exercises in Composition

(1) Add two inner voices (alto and tenor). You will notice that the soprano is *diatonic* and the bass is *chromatic,* except at the cadence which has been strengthened by fifth-related tones. Considering the chromaticism of the bass line, some chords of embellishment (without root function) might be in order. Be sure to group your chords carefully; remember that triads generally serve better as resolutions of sevenths than the reverse. Analyze thoroughly.

(2) Add two or three voices below this soprano line. The melody is rather *chromatic,* but should be harmonized with essentially *diatonic* harmony, i.e. *every chord should have a functional root.* Secondary dominants, augmented sixth chords, and Neapolitan sixths usually have functional roots (V or IV function), and may be regarded, therefore, as in the province of diatonic harmony even though they contain chromatically altered tones. It follows that some of the chromatic tones in the melody below will be part of such chords, while the other chromatic tones will be nonharmonic tones. Chromatic chords of embellishment, characteristic in a chromatic style, should *not* be used *here.* Compare this style with that of the first exercise, above. Analyze thoroughly.

(3) Add two inner parts. Both the soprano and the bass engage in chromatic activity. Be sure to observe the points of harmonic rest (indicated by a comma) by using chords of resolution. The restful chords should be preceded by chords having greater harmonic tension. Note the enharmonic change in measure 2, the sequence in measures 3-4, and the *suggestion* of another sequence in measure 5.

The success of your writing will depend to a large extent upon the logic of your voice leading, the sense of continuing harmonic and rhythmic momentum, and the ebb and flow of harmonic tension and resolution. Try to limit your chromatic chords of embellishment to (a) triads, (b) seventh chords (preferably dominant, diminished, or half-diminished in structure), and (c) augmented sixth chords. Indicate the point of modulation in your analysis.

Supplementary Exercises

(a) Sing at sight several modulating and nonmodulating chromatic melodies. Analyze each first to determine the point of modulation.

(b) Dictation of chromatic melodies and harmonic progressions.

(c) Using a bass line similar to that in the first exercise (chromatic descending, concluding with II-V-I) and an ascending diatonic soprano line, improvise at the keyboard the following modulations:

    (1) From C minor to E minor

    (2) From E major to B♭ major

    (3) From G major to D major

    (Suggestion: Play the bass line alone first, then the bass and soprano lines, finally in four-part harmony.)

(d) Harmonize the melody of Exercise (3) above, using the following bass line:

XXVI

Turn-of-the-Century Developments (Part One)

The music we have analyzed thus far lends itself to collective systematic study because at the time it was written there existed a common practice, a general contemporaneous agreement regarding harmonic propriety, dissonance usage, and so forth, that transcended individual idiosyncracies or personal styles.

Music composed since about 1890 is in general more stylized, more idiosyncratic and exclusive than that composed before 1890, and the many musical styles that have evolved in the 20th century have so far resisted all efforts to unify them. There is no common practice in contemporary music.

Since this more recent music does not lend itself easily to the traditionally systematic approach to musical theory, the only remaining avenue would seem to be the historical, in which the student (1) examines each of the various styles and techniques side by side, (2) recognizes their novel elements, (3) reconciles their differences where possible, (4) relates each style to principles already established in the great mainstream of music, and (5) attempts to penetrate the logic and musical reasonableness behind the apparently willful.

Four composers have been chosen to illustrate just a few of the important developments that have taken place in the last half-century or so. Each composer has made notable contributions to our thinking about harmony, melody, counterpoint, form, and so on. Each has provided his answer to the question "Where do we go from here?" Whether or not one agrees with the answers of Debussy, Ravel, Richard Strauss, and Scriabin, at least one must recognize the challenge of their thought, the persuasiveness of their music. Music is different today for their having lived and created, and it behooves us, as their musical descendants, to study their work and relate it both to the more remote past and to current practice. Only through such activity can there be continuity of culture and further development of a complex art.

CLAUDE DEBUSSY (1862–1918) AND MAURICE RAVEL (1875–1937)

These two composers are commonly linked together (like Bach and Handel, Haydn and Mozart, etc.), yet they have quite different compositional styles. However, they do employ a reasonably similar harmonic vocabulary and syntax, as the two excerpts which follow clearly show. These works are products of both composers' earlier years and, although representative pieces, do not show the more radical differences that might be found in comparing their later compositions. The most important style characteristics to be found in the Debussy and Ravel excerpts are discussed below.

Modality. The major and minor modes, although not abandoned, retire in favor of the ecclesiastical modes. This may be seen in the melodic lines, harmonic progressions, and particularly at the cadences where the leading tone and the dominant function are conspicuously absent. In this style the conventional cadence forms seldom appear; modal cadences more frequently take their place. There are occasional suggestions of the pentatonic scale.* (See Ex. I, mm. 2–3, 14–16; Ex. II, mm. 13–18, where the melody is based upon the scale F♯-G♯-A♯-C♯-E♯.)

Chord Forms.

(1) Triads used in these examples are either major or minor. No augmented or diminished triads appear. (The augmented triads that are so prominent a feature in some of Debussy's music are usually correlated with a melodic use of the whole tone scale† in which all the thirds are major.)

---

* Cf. Vol. I, Ch. II, Ex. I (*a*).

† Cf. Vol. I, Ch. II, Ex. I (*d*).

(2) Seventh chords are sometimes dominant, but minor and half-diminished seventh chords are more common in Debussy, especially in the modal passages. All three types may be found in Examples I and II, and other forms of the seventh chord may be found elsewhere in these composers' works. The diminished seventh chord is rather rare in this style.

(3) Ninth and thirteenth chords are all dominant in structure. The eleventh chord does not appear in these examples.

(4) Not previously encountered in our studies are the triads with added tones. The coloristic added second ($+2$) or added sixth ($+6$), counting the intervals above the chord root, is applied only to a triad and not to a seventh or more dissonant chord.

   (a) The triad with added sixth (T^{+6} or t^{+6}) is an outgrowth of the seventh chord in first inversion (the six-five chord) which it resembles in structure but not in function. The root of the six-five chord corresponds to the added sixth in a triad, but the former (as a structural tone) functions quite differently from the latter (which is decorative). Likewise the seventh of the chord (in a six-five) is a dissonance in need of resolution, but the corresponding tone in a triad with added sixth is the fifth of the chord, which is free to move without restraint. Finally, the root of the triad with added sixth is usually in the bass voice rather than in an upper voice, necessarily the case with the six-five chord. (See Ex. I, meas. 14; Ex. II, mm. 13, 24.)

   (b) The triad with added second (T^{+2} or t^{+2}) evolved from the ninth chord. Since the former presupposes the absence of a chord-seventh and the latter assumes the presence of a chord-seventh, there is usually no danger of confusing the two (see Ex. II, mm. 27–29). Ravel is particularly fond (although this is not shown in the present example) of the triad with an added minor second ($T^{+\flat 2}$ or $t^{+\flat 2}$), which suggests an appoggiatura sounded simultaneously with its resolution. Precedent for this procedure may be found in some of the sonatas of Domenico Scarlatti (see discussion of "harmonic superposition" in Ralph Kirkpatrick, *Domenico Scarlatti,* Princeton University Press, Princeton, 1953, pp. 229–36), and in the harmonic style of the Cante Hondo (flamenco) which is based on the Phrygian mode and customarily cadences with 4-♭3-♭2-1 (A-G-F-E).

Chord Progressions. A string or chain of seventh or ninth chords is not uncommon. When these move in parallel motion (the customary procedure) there is usually an absence of the traditional resolutions of the chord-seventh and chord-ninth, except perhaps at the end of the series. Such a group may include chords of the same structure (more frequent) or of slightly varying structure; parallel triads, seventh, and ninth chords are all permitted. They remind one of medieval parallel organum, and sound quite at home in the setting provided by the ecclesiastical modes. (See Ex. I, mm. 15-16; Ex. II, mm. 1-5, 11-14.)

Parallel octaves, revived from medieval practice, are found in Example I, measures 8 and 15-16, between the voice and the bass lines, and in Example II at measures 1–5. Parallel fifths may be seen in Example I at measures 6–8 in the bass, and in Example II at measures 13–18 and 23–29, also in the bass.

Bass Progressions. The interval of a second or third as a bass progression appears more frequently than the perfect fourth or fifth, even at cadences. The IV-V-I progression in Example I (mm. 8-9) involves a minor V, making it a modal cadence rather than a conventional authentic cadence. The strongest cadences in Example I (mm. 7-8 and 13-14) use a stepwise bass. However, there is a regular tonal cadence (V-I) at measures 13-14. It is followed by a short extension or closing member of three measures that obviously returns to a modal style.

Spacing and Doubling. No complete set of rules can be offered to the student with respect to chord spacing and the doubling of chord tones. The two following examples should be examined carefully. Play them at the piano, listening attentively. Note, for example: the open spacing employed by Debussy in Example I, at measures 11-13 and 17, the close spacing in the upper register, with the melody doubled in the bass in the opening measures of Example II. Note further Ravel's rather consistent use of chords in root position, with the seventh and ninth in the upper part of the chord; and so forth.

Irregular Resolutions. Occasionally chord-sevenths and -ninths resolve up instead of down, are held over as common tones in the next chord, or are left unresolved when they appear in a series of chords that progress in parallel motion. (See Ex. I, meas. 7; Ex. II, almost constantly.)

Chords of Embellishment. Chords similar to those described in Volume II, Chapter XIII, are found in Example I, measure 12 (between the two V chords), measures 15-16 (between the F♯ chords), and in Example II at measures 13-14 (where the A♯ and C♯ triads function as lower and upper neighbor chords to the B chord) and measures 27-28 (where the enharmonic A minor triad is an embellishment of the F♯ chord).

Nonharmonic Tones. The familiar types are found; they resolve in the customary way. Both illustrations should be analyzed thoroughly with respect to nonharmonic tone usage.

Modulatory Procedures. Modulations must be studied in terms of established key centers, which are sometimes a little vague, as at the beginning of Example I, or at measures 18-19 of Example II. Doubtful areas are usually extensions of nontonic harmony (tonicizations), and in retrospect may be seen as directly related to the subsequent tonal (key) objective. Modulatory devices are of the types already discussed.

The Final Chord. This may be:

    (a) a triad;

    (b) a seventh chord—usually minor or major in structure, since I^7 in the major mode is a major seventh chord and I^7 in the minor mode is a minor seventh chord. It is obviously impractical to expect any other type of seventh chord to assume a tonic function.

    (c) a triad with an added second or sixth (possibly, though rarely, both). The last chord in the complete work of which Example I is only the first part is a major triad with an added sixth (T^{+6}). Example II ends on a major triad with an added second (T^{+2}).

The student should examine all the principal cadences in order to ascertain the chord structures used for phrase endings.

Example I. "En Sourdine" (First Part) by Claude Debussy.*

_____

* The text is omitted. By permission, International Music Co., New York, and Jean Jobert & Cie, Paris.

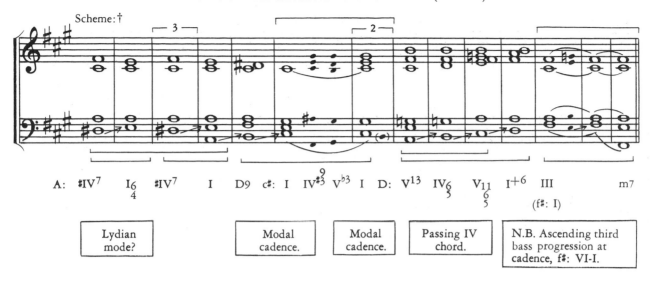

A: $\sharp IV^7$ I^6_4 $\sharp IV^7$ I   D9   c$\sharp$: I $IV^{\sharp 3}_9$ $V^{\flat 3}$ I   D: V^{13} IV^6_5 $V_{11 \atop 6 \atop 5}$ I^{+6} III   m7

(f$\sharp$: I)

| Lydian mode? | | Modal cadence. | Modal cadence. | Passing IV chord. | N.B. Ascending third bass progression at cadence, f$\sharp$: VI-I. |

Example II. Sonatine (First Movement, Last Part) by Maurice Ravel.*

(Modéré)

mp très expressif

ppp subito

mf

---

† Brackets indicate harmonic group or prolongation. Figure above staff indicates measures in the original. See p. 92 for key to abbreviations
* Permission to reprint granted by Durand & Cie, Paris, copyright owners; and by Elkan-Vogel Co., Inc., Philadelphia, Pa., agents.

Scheme: *

* See p. 92 for key to abbreviations.

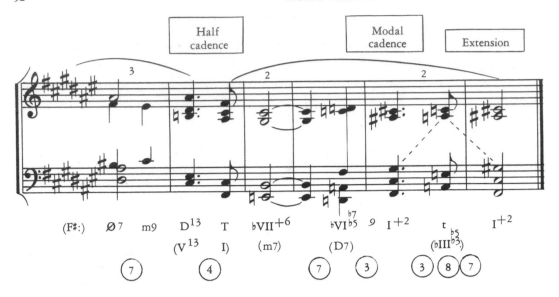

Key to abbreviations in the analysis:

T   (major triad)
t   (minor triad)
+2   (with added second)
+6   (with added sixth)
D7, D9   (dominant seventh/ninth)
m7, m9   (minor seventh/ninth)
Ø7   (half-diminished seventh)
(1) Chord embellished by double appoggiaturas resolving in parallel fifths.
(2) Chord embellished by ninth-like appoggiatura.
(3) Root progression of an ascending third.
(4) Fifth relationship in bass (root) progression.
(5) Embellished by N.T.
(6) Embellished by Double N.T.
(7) Rhythmic motive ♪♫ or (♪) ♫♪
(8) Neighboring chord—compare Example VI, Chapter XXVIII. Review discussion in Chapter XIII.

Figures above the staff refer to the number of measures in the original.

SUGGESTED EXERCISES

(a) Analyze the preceding Debussy and Ravel examples measure by measure and phrase by phrase. Use the style characteristics discussed above as a check list.

(b) Write a short composition for piano and solo string or woodwind instrument, using the harmonic structure of the Debussy example as given. Employ ¢ meter and one of the following suggested beginnings. Use a fairly consistent texture and style throughout.

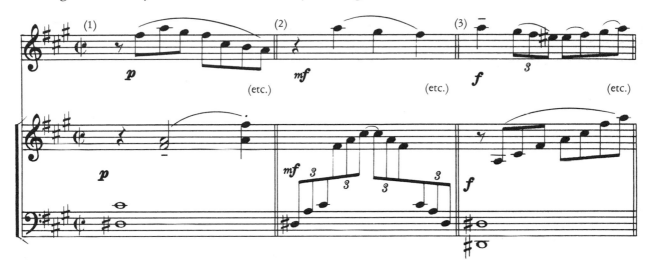

(c) Keyboard exercises:

  (1) Harmonize ascending and descending scales in the Dorian, Phrygian, Lydian, and Mixolydian modes as follows:

  (*a*) using parallel triads;
  (*b*) using triads, with a bass line generally in contrary motion to the soprano;
  (*c*) using parallel seventh chords, in root position and inverted;
  (*d*) using a free combination of triads, sevenths, ninths, and thirteenths.

  (2) Play four parallel, dominant ninth chords; progress from the last of these to a tonic triad with added sixth or added second.

  (3) Play the following in each of the modes listed in (1) above. If necessary, use B♭ or F♯ to avoid the tritone (i.e., avoid the diminished triad), but observe the effect on the mode.

```
I  IV  V    I          I  V  IV  I
I  VI  III  I          I  V  VI  I
```

XXVII

Exercises in Composition

Using as a guide the principles discussed in the last chapter, and with the Debussy and Ravel examples as models, harmonize the following soprano and bass lines. Analyze thoroughly.

In (1) fill in the harmony as directed, using the chord types indicated above the soprano (see pp. 68 and 92 for a review of the meaning of the symbols employed). All the chords are in root position; they will, in some cases, have more than four parts (voices). Supply additional root analysis under the bass where necessary.

In working out (2) you should add inner voices. Choose chord types within the following limits:

   (a) *triads,* major or minor, with or without added second *or* sixth;

   (b) *sevenths* of the familiar variety, preference going to dominant, half-diminished, major, and minor sevenths (avoid the diminished);

   (c) dominant *ninths* and *thirteenths.*

SUPPLEMENTARY EXERCISES

(a) Practice (1) at the keyboard, using the given outer voices and suggested harmonies. Improvise another version, using different chords.

(b) Practice singing the above soprano and bass lines, concentrating on intervals. If the inner voices are worked out sing them also, individually. Then sing the entire example as a four- or five-part chorus. Transpose the bass notes up an octave if they go below your vocal range.

(c) Dictation of correlated melodic and harmonic materials.

(d) Perform in class the student compositions suggested in Chapter XXVI, Exercise (b).

XXVIII

Turn-of-the-Century Developments (Part Two)

RICHARD STRAUSS (1864–1949)

The music of this stylistic descendant of Wagner and Brahms extends harmonic syntax in many new and bold directions. We will consider here a few of the more important of these.

Examples I (from "Der Rosenkavalier") and II (the final measures of "Don Quixote") show how Strauss uses familiar triads and seventh chords in such a way as to provide an element of mild shock or surprise. The effect is achieved through the use of chords whose roots are quite remote from each other, from the prevailing tonal center, or both. These chords (and their connection) may be justified or explained by such extenuating circumstances as (a) the familiar sound of the individual chords as vertical structures, (b) the use of one or more common tones (not uncommonly enharmonic equivalents), (c) parallelism (such as we have seen in the works of Debussy and Ravel), or (d) what might be described as deceptive but stepwise voice leading to an unexpected chord. Sometimes the effect on the listener is of being led astray, rather playfully perhaps; one feels like the innocent victim of a very sophisticated prankster. The deception is all in jest, the rule-breaking a momentary madcap, for the ultimate resolution is inevitably orthodox, conventional, and morally upright.

Example I begins on IV in E major and ends on V^7 (which ultimately reaches I). Between the IV and the V^7 Strauss has placed three root position major triads that seem to have little connection with the key or with their neighbors although C is V of F. There is a sequential relationship, A:C::F:Ab, that involves root progression to the minor mediants of A (E:IV) and F (E:N6) respectively. The remoteness is emphasized by several cross relations. Note the enharmonic change Eb-D#.

Example I. Excerpt from "Der Rosenkavalier."*

Example II is an elaborated VI^7-V^7-I cadence. The embellishing and quite remote dominant sevenths move in parallel motion in all voices but the soprano. The Ab in measure 3 is heard as an enharmonic G#. As a result the Bb-Ab progression in measures 2-3 is heard as a diminished third. Note the orthodox final resolution.

---

* "Der Rosenkavalier" by Richard Strauss, copyright 1912 by Adolph Furstner, Paris; copyright renewed 1940 by Furstner, Ltd., London; copyright assigned 1943 to Boosey & Hawkes, Ltd., London; excerpt reprinted by permission.

Example II. Excerpt from "Don Quixote."

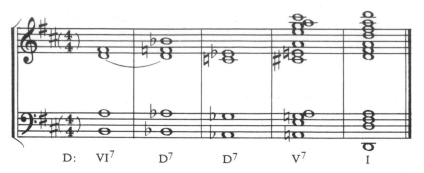

Examples III to VII (from "Elektra")* reveal some of the characteristics noted above. We see further:

(1) The use of parallel tritones in contrary motion in Example III. The embellishing, nonfunctional augmented sixth chords (French sixth) between the dagger signs (†) constitute a formal extension and illustrate the neighboring chord principle. The state of dynamic equilibrium achieved by this prolongation could last indefinitely. Strauss brings the progression to a halt by resolving the last augmented sixth chord to a B minor six-four chord. This moves chromatically (sideslip) to another six-four (an orthodox tonic six-four), V^7, and I in B♭ minor. The vocal part is omitted.

(2) The extreme use of distantly related triads and sevenths, similar to those in Examples I and II, but more extended and protracted or less justified by voice-leading considerations, may be seen in Examples IV and V. An occasional unresolved dissonance appears, the expected note of resolution of which (1) may appear in another voice, or (2) may have *preceded* the note in question. When quitted by a wide leap this dissonance is referred to as an "*escaped tone*" (compare the échappée). The text is omitted in the vocal parts.

(3) The last two chords of the opera illustrate again the close association of two chords whose roots and keys are quite remote from each other. Stepwise motion is the chief connective factor (see Ex. VI).

(4) Modulation to a remote key through the use of parallel, chromatically related, dominant seventh chords, embellished by suspensions, the outer voices in parallel octaves as in Example VII. Compare the procedure with that in Example III. The text is omitted in the vocal part.

Example III. Excerpt (♯1) from "Elektra."*

---

* "Elektra" by Richard Strauss, copyright 1909, 1910 by Adolph Furstner, Paris; copyright renewed 1937 by Furstner, Ltd. London; copyright assigned 1943 to Boosey & Hawkes, Ltd.; excerpts reprinted by permission.

† Same chord as in measure 9 (enharmonic equivalent).

Example IV. Excerpt (♯2) from "Elektra."*

---

† Same chord as in measure 1 (enharmonic equivalent).

* "Elektra" by Richard Strauss, copyright 1909, 1910 by Adolph Furstner, Paris; copyright renewed 1937 by Furstner, Ltd. London; copyright assigned 1943 to Boosey & Hawkes, Ltd.; excerpts reprinted by permission.

Example V. Excerpt (♯3) from "Elektra."*

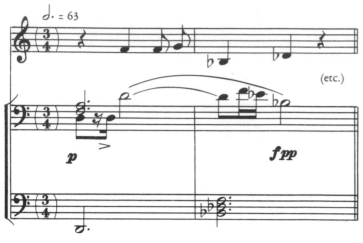

Example VI. Excerpt (♯4) from "Elektra."*

Example VII. Excerpt (♯5) from "Elektra."*

SUGGESTED EXERCISES

(a) Using "disassociated" major or minor triads and dominant seventh chords, harmonize the following progressions. Upper case (F) indicates major triad or dominant seventh chord. Lower case (f) indicates minor triad.

    (1) Play each chord separately at the piano. Then play the outer voices. Finally, play the entire progression in an even tempo.

* "Elektra" by Richard Strauss, copyright 1909, 1910 by Adolph Furstner, Paris; copyright renewed 1937 by Furstner, Ltd. London; copyright assigned 1943 to Boosey & Hawkes, Ltd.; excerpts reprinted by permission.

(2) Play the melody alone first. Then play again, adding a suitable bass line. Finally, add inner voices and play in an even tempo.

Bb: I   (Not V)   I

(b) Dictation of harmonic progressions similar to those suggested above.

(c) Sing the following melodies.

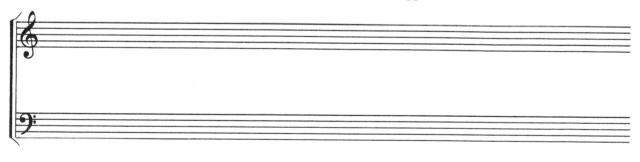

(d) Provide written harmonizations for two of the melodies that appear under (c) above.

XXIX

Turn-of-the-Century Developments (Part Three)

ALEXANDER SCRIABIN (1872–1915)

The very strong and individual harmonic elements of this composer's music overshadow the melodic and contrapuntal to a degree almost without equal in musical history. The work of Scriabin should be viewed as one of the last great outbursts of the romantic 19th century which was so strongly attracted by the expressive possibilities of harmonic coloring.

Melodic style. The heptatonic (seven-note) diatonic scale is abandoned in favor of the dodecatonic (twelve-note) chromatic scale. In the latter system no chromatic alteration is possible since all notes are equal members of the scale; C and C♯ are two different notes and not chromatic variants of the same scale degree. In Scriabin the melody does not seem derived from any scale, diatonic or chromatic, and is sometimes hardly distinguishable from harmonic figuration. As one might expect in a harmonically oriented style, the texture is chiefly homophonic.

Tonality. The tonal center is elusive (again we see some early roots of the later Schoenberg twelve-tone theory), since the leading tone function tends to disappear where all scale steps are half-steps. Tonic and dominant functions disappear too. Tritones, which traditionally are ambiguous, are very common in Scriabin and acquire a neutral value because of their indecisiveness and lack of conventional resolution. They create a sense of rudderless floating in a vast musical space where there is no gravitational pull. The dynamic equilibrium is maintained (1) by deliberate avoidance of resolution into chords that would have lower harmonic tension, and (2) by an apparently endless chain of chords containing the tritone interval. (Compare Ex. III in Ch. XXVIII.)

Chord forms. The so-called "mystic chord" of Scriabin* is only one of many similarly constructed chords. They all seem related to the eleventh and thirteenth chords in complexity and number of tones, but in their emphasis upon the interval of the fourth they foreshadow the quartal harmonies (chords built upon successive fourths)† that flourish in much contemporary music (e.g. Hindemith). The favored chords contain not only perfect fourths (most prevalent) but augmented and diminished fourths as well. Open spacing emphasizing the unfilled intervals of the fourth and the minor seventh is preferred.

Chord connections. Still noticeable is the seemingly eternal preference for common tones and stepwise motion with a minimum of leaps. Leaps in all or many voices are confined generally to chords moving in parallel motion (as in Debussy and Ravel) where the chord structures are the same or similar.

The first part of the "Poëme," opus 69, no. 1, is given on the following pages together with a reduction showing the underlying harmonic framework both in traditional terms (tertial chords) and in terms of quartal harmony. Note the comparative infrequency of nonharmonic tones and the fluid motion from one chord to another with little variation in tension level. Observe voice leading, common tones, bass line, and so forth.

---

* See further the article on Scriabin (Skriabin) in *Grove's Dictionary of Music and Musicians,* 5th ed.
† See Vol. I, Ch. XI, Ex. II.

Example I. Excerpt (Opening Measures) from "Poëme," Opus 69, No. 1, by Scriabin.

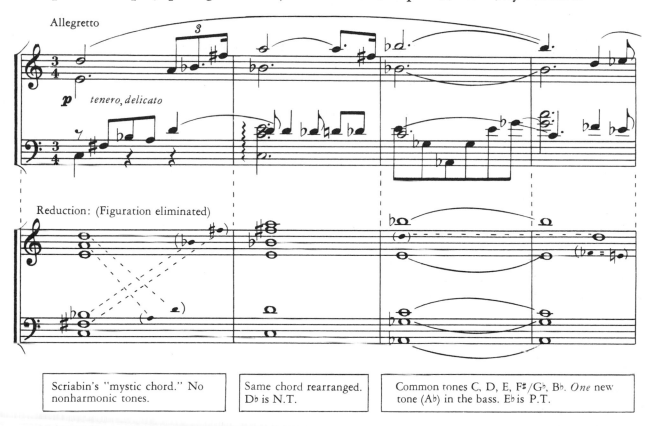

Scriabin's "mystic chord." No nonharmonic tones.	Same chord rearranged. D♭ is N.T.	Common tones C, D, E, F♯/G♭, B♭. *One* new tone (A♭) in the bass. E♭ is P.T.

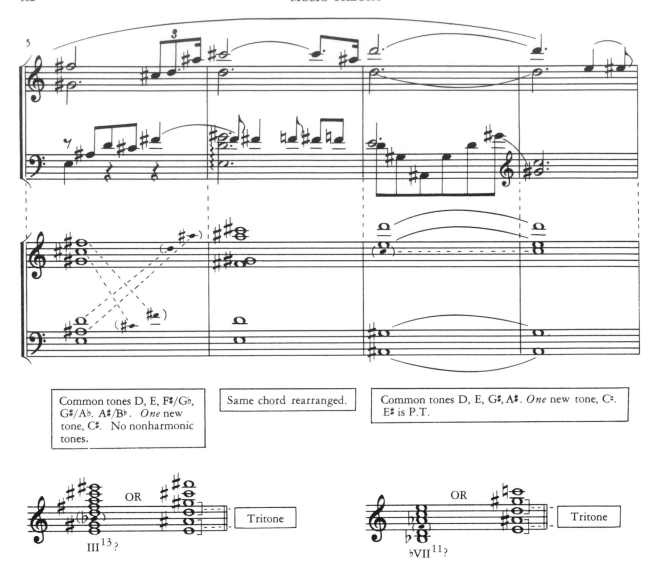

Common tones D, E, F♯/G♭, G♯/A♭, A♯/B♭. *One* new tone, C♯. No nonharmonic tones.

Same chord rearranged.

Common tones D, E, G♯, A♯. *One* new tone, C♮. E♯ is P.T.

III¹³ ?

Tritone

♭VII¹¹ ?

Tritone

| Common tones D, E, G♯. *Two* new tones for the beginning of the new phrase, C♯, F♯. F♯ is P.T. | Only *one* common tone, C♯. Parallel motion, similar construction. D♯ an inverted Ech. | Repetition of two previous measures. Anacrusis is omitted. |

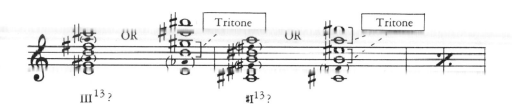

One common tone, D♯. The new tones are reached by half-step motion. No nonharmonic tones.

Tritone

I^{13}?

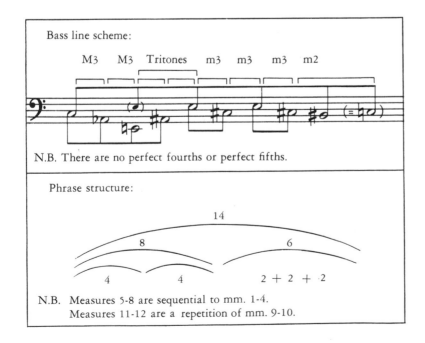

Bass line scheme:

M3　M3　Tritones　m3　m3　m3　m2

N.B. There are no perfect fourths or perfect fifths.

Phrase structure:

14

8　　　　　　6

4　　4　　　2 + 2 + 2

N.B.　Measures 5-8 are sequential to mm. 1-4.
　　　Measures 11-12 are a repetition of mm. 9-10.

SUGGESTED EXERCISES

(a) Harmonize the following, using the given lines as outer voices. Employ escaped tones and irregularly resolved seventh chords where indicated. Use the style characteristics of Richard Strauss discussed in the previous chapter. The examples there may serve as a guide.

Abbreviations: (1) escaped tone.

(2) irregularly resolved seventh chord.

(continued)

(b) Using the Scriabin example as a model, and following the stylistic principles discussed in this chapter, write a musical phrase based upon the following harmonic scheme.

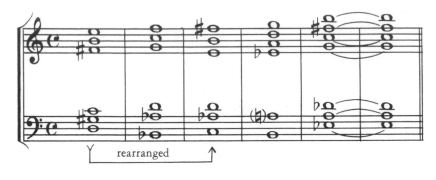

Bass line intervals:

M3　　　M2　　　m2　　　Enh.
down　　up　　　down　　M3 up

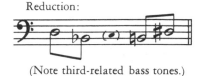

Reduction:

(Note third-related bass tones.)

(c) Dictation of materials related to the subject of this and the preceding chapter.

(d) Each student should play at the piano his realization of the above composition exercises.

(e) Sing chromatic melodies such as the following (based on (b) above). Suggestion: sustain the given chords on the piano as an accompaniment to the voice during the first reading; additional readings should be without such harmonic support.

XXX

Final Project

The final project may be either an analytical study or an original composition. Preliminary discussion of student plans should take place at least a week before the last class meeting. The project should reveal the full measure of comprehension and insight achieved by the student to date. It should further display a just balance between imagination and self-discipline.

Option A: Analytical Study.

A work of about two or three pages of piano music (or the equivalent) in length, chosen by the student and approved by the instructor, should be analyzed thoroughly. The study should be intensive and comprehensive; it should reveal not only a capacity to label chords properly but also an awareness of such elements as repetition, variation, sequence, embellishment, extension, modulation, and so forth. Phrase or periodic structures and cadences should be recognized. A reduction, similar to those already presented as illustrations, should be submitted along with the analysis. Nonharmonic tones should be identified, irregularities of usage accounted for, and something should be said about the style of the work under investigation.

Option B: Study in Composition.

The student should submit either a melodic, bass, harmonic, formal, or other plan for a composition of at least 30–50 measures. After the instructor has approved the plan, the student should complete the work without further assistance. The work should be in a style which is consistent and one which has been covered in this course. The music should be analyzed thoroughly, as suggested in Option A above. The work may be scored for such instrumental and/or vocal resources as are available, and should be played at the final class meeting. It is suggested that the instructor discuss briefly some of the problems that may arise in the copying of parts—such as the need for rehearsal numbers or letters, cues, slurs and phrasing, dynamics, tempo indications, and so forth. He should discuss transposition, clefs, ranges, etc. with the individual student in need of such assistance.

APPENDIX

Selected Examples for Analysis and Class Discussion

EXAMPLE A Arcangelo Corelli (1653–1713). Sonata in D major for two violins and continuo. First movement.*

---

* Figured bass indications have been omitted.

1. Where (indicate measure and beat) do the cadences appear, what kind are they (perfect authentic, half), and in what key?

2. What evidence of thematic unity do you find?

3. What are the most frequently used nonharmonic tones? Locate several illustrations of each.

4. Compare the prepared seventh chords with the suspensions.

5. What is the modulatory scheme of this movement?

6. Where are the "pivot" or common chords (at the points of modulation)?

7. Are there any instances of the use of sequence? imitation?

8. What is the function of the C♮ in measure 17?

9. Are there any embellished resolutions of nonharmonic tones? Where? Describe them.

10. Discuss the rhythmic structure and balance of the phrases, noting the distribution of moving parts among the several voices and the approaches to the cadences.

———

EXAMPLE B Johann Sebastian Bach (1685–1750). Partita in B minor for unaccompanied violin. Sarabande and Double (Variation).

* The "Double" is a variation of the preceding dance movement. See the article on "Double," par. 1, in *Grove's Dictionary of Music and Musicians,* 5th ed.

112

1. What is the harmonic and phrase structure of measures 1–8 of the Sarabande? Compare the Double (mm. 1–8).

2. Where are the cadences, what form are they, and in what key?

3. What is the modulatory scheme? Compare the previous Corelli example.

4. Compare the Double with the Sarabande beat by beat, noting the harmonic parallelism, melodic relationships, the occasional use of different embellishments, etc.

5. What are the three-voice implications in the single line melody of the Double? Write a strict three voice setting based on the principal tones of the Double; continue as suggested in footnote† below.

6. What are the voice leading implications in the Sarabande, not altogether explicit in the music as written, but logically necessary and "understood" in terms of strict part writing?

7. What similarities and what differences can you find in comparing the variation technique exhibited by Bach here and by Beethoven in Example F?

8. What nonharmonic tones are implied in the Double?

9. Compare the rhythmic properties of the Sarabande and the Double.

10. What harmonic "irregularities" are to be found in:
    (a) Sarabande, measures 8, 11-12, 29?
    (b) Double, measures 3-4?
    Explain or justify the procedures.

11. Where are there examples of:
    (a) the harmonic minor mode?
    (b) the ascending form of the melodic minor mode in a descending progression?

(etc.)

EXAMPLE C Domenico Scarlatti (1685–1757). Sonata in F minor (Longo 187, Kirkpatrick 481). First half.*

* See Vol. II, Ch. IV, Ex. II, for a detailed analysis of the first eight measures. See Kirkpatrick, Appendix IV, for comments on the signs of ornamentation.

1. Where (indicate measure and beat) do the cadences appear, what kind are they (perfect authentic, half), and in what key?

2. Where do you find examples of phrase extension through the use of a deceptive cadence? An evaded cadence? (See Vol. I, Ch. XXVII, for definition and illustration of these terms.)

3. Compare the upward- and the downward-resolving appoggiaturas, observing such matters as length of the dissonant tone, length of resolution, notation, etc.

4. What is the effect upon the harmonic rhythm of the long descending arpeggios in measures 21-2 and 24-5?

5. What types of nonharmonic tones are created by the syncopation in measures 6, 13–16, 18?

6. Where is there a curious instance of parallel octaves?

7. What evidence of motivic or thematic unity do you find?

8. What is the modulatory scheme?

9. Compare the texture with the previous Corelli example.

10. What is the harmonically structural function of measures 20–27 and 27–35? In what matters are they similar? Dissimilar?

EXAMPLE D Wolfgang Amadeus Mozart (1756–91). Concerto in A major for Piano and Orchestra (Köchel 488). Second movement, measures 53–68.

Questions and Problems

1. How many phrases are there in this excerpt? Identify the cadences.

2. Discuss the several devices used by Mozart for the purpose of phrase extension.

3. What term would describe the form of this selection?

4. Discuss the harmonic rhythm, noting particularly the pattern in measure 54.

5. What motivic or thematic elements help provide formal unity?

6. Compare the texture with that of the previous Corelli and Scarlatti examples.

7. What nonharmonic tones are used?

8. Discuss the chromatic alterations found in measures 58 and 60 (note the major-minor mixture) and 65-6 in terms of approach, resolution, effect on chord structure and tonality, etc.

9. Where do you find examples of melodic embellishment? an arpeggio? an expressive melodic leap? a Neapolitan sixth chord?

10. Explain the change of chord in measure 58, the D♯ in the bass, and the harmonic minor mode in the soprano in measure 59. Relate the harmonic procedures used in measures 58 and 60.

EXAMPLE E Wolfgang Amadeus Mozart. Gigue for Piano, (Köchel 574). First half.

QUESTIONS AND PROBLEMS

1. Compare the texture with that of the previous examples. Discuss the use of imitation.

2. Discuss the small formal divisions, their internal structure, their relationship to each other thematically, and their function in the larger form.

3. What is the modulatory scheme?

4. Discuss thoroughly the use of secondary dominants and chromatic alteration generally.

5. Where are there definite cadences? suggestions of cadence? What type are they?

6. Discuss the nonharmonic tones. Note particularly the suggestion of an inverted pedal point in measures 12–14.

EXAMPLE F Ludwig van Beethoven (1770–1827). "Diabelli" Variations, Opus 120. The Theme, and Variation No. III.

Var. III [Poco allegro]

1. What is the phrase structure of the Theme? Where are the cadences? What type are they, and in what key?

2. Discuss the use of secondary dominants and the principle of harmonic prolongation in the Theme.

3. How does Beethoven make the accent on the third beat an important structural element in the Theme?

4. Discuss the textures of both Theme and Variation. Note particularly the occasional "irregularities" in part writing, and the implications of the wide leaps in connection with both part writing and the phrase structure.

5. Compare the harmonic structure of the Theme with that of the Variation. Discuss any evidence of the chord substitution principle.

6. What elements of polyphonic texture and of motivic development are present in Variation III?

7. Explain the relationship of the following elements in Variation III:

   (a) the harmony of measures 20 (third beat) through 25 (first beat),
   (b) the chord on the second beat of measure 25.

8. Where are there examples of the augmented sixth chord? of chromatic nonharmonic tones?

9. Compare the modulatory scheme of the Theme with that of the Variation.

10. Compare the binary form with that of the Bach Partita movement (Ex. B in the Appendix, above). Compare also the variation techniques of the two composers.

* The text of the song has been omitted.

QUESTIONS AND PROBLEMS

1. Compare the harmonic structure of measures 1-2, 3-4, and 25–7.

2. Discuss the major-minor alternations in measures 6, 9, 12 29-30, and 33-4. Is the D chord in measure 14 a tonic chord in D major, or is it an example of the Picardy third?

3. Discuss the apparent modulations at measures 10–13 and 17–25, observing the significance of the cadences and the thematic recurrence at measure 25. What techniques are used to make reference to distant keys without a real modulation?

4. Where is there an example of enharmonic change? Why is it used?

5. What is the phrase structure of the song? How are the phrases related to each other in terms of key, cadence form, length, texture, thematic materials, etc.?

6. Discuss the texture of the piano accompaniment, the spacing and doubling of chord tones, the relationship of the piano to the voice part.

7. Where is there an augmented sixth chord? a Neapolitan sixth chord?

8. What types of nonharmonic tones are there?

9. Compare this song with the one by Hugo Wolf (Ex. J). List the factors in outline form.

10. Compare this example of three-part form with the Schumann and Chopin illustrations (Ex. H and I). List the factors in outline form.

EXAMPLE H Robert Schumann (1810–56). "Carnaval," Opus 9. Valse Noble.

1. What is the plan or idea behind the bass line in measures 1–8 and 26–40, and how does it compare with the plan of the bass in measures 9–25?

2. Where are the principal cadences, what forms are they, and how are they related to the thematic materials employed?

3. Compare the use of chromatic passing and neighboring tones (nonharmonic tones) with the chromatic chord tones.

4. Discuss the formal design of the whole, and examine carefully the phrase structure of each of the three parts.

5. How is the textural plan related to the form?

6. What is the evidence in behalf of a change of key in the middle section, and what is the evidence against it? What is your decision?

7. Are there any chromatically altered chords in this work that do *not* fall into the secondary dominant category?

8. Explain the necessity for the enharmonic change in measures 24-5.

9. Explain the D in measure 39, second half of the third beat.

10. Why did Schumann not end the piece at measure 32? Would it not have been a logical point at which to stop since it matches measure 8? Why did he continue, and what is the function of the added eight measures?

EXAMPLE I Frederic Chopin (1810–49). Mazurka in F minor, Opus 63, No. 2.

1. Compare the first eight measures of this composition with the corresponding measures of the Schumann work quoted in Example H. Compare measures 1–16 with measures 1–8 of the Schumann.

2. What further similarities and what differences can you find in the handling of three-part form, texture, phrase structure, over-all modulatory scheme, harmonic vocabulary, dissonance usage, chromaticism, chord spacing, and so forth, in comparing the two works?

3. Where do the principal cadences appear? What type are they, and in what key?

4. What evidence of thematic unity can you find?

5. Discuss the phrase structures, noting particularly (a) the use of parallel (or partially repeated) phrases, (b) similar or dissimilar cadences, (c) evidence of period structure, and so forth.

6. Where does Chopin use ninth chords? Are they all dominant ninths (in structure and function)? How are the chords spaced? What notes are doubled? Does the chord appear in any positions other than root and first inversion?

7. Account for the chromatically altered tones in measures 7, 16, 18, 53, 55, 56. Identify the name and explain the function of each.

8. What pronounced rhythmic characteristic (common to many mazurkas) helps to relate the "A" and "B" sections of this three part form?*

9. How does Chopin achieve an unusual modulatory effect in his return to the original key?

10. What is the formal function of measures 33–40?

---

* See *Grove's Dictionary of Music and Musicians,* 5th ed., the article on "Mazurka," for a discussion of the special rhythmic properties of this Polish dance form.

EXAMPLE J.   Hugo Wolf (1860–1903). "Bescheidene Liebe" ("Modest Heart").*

Questions and Problems

1. What is the phrase structure of this song? Which phrases are closely related, what is their relationship to each other, and which are contrasting phrases? Is there evidence of period form? Compare cadences and keys.

2. Compare the textures of the several phrases, noting the relationship of texture to form.

3. What is the special function of the last four measures, and why is it *mf* instead of *pp?*

4. Discuss the use of secondary dominants.

5. Why do the B-flats in measures 9 and 11 resolve upward to B-natural instead of down to A?

6. What differences are there in the harmonization and the melodic line in measures 13–16 as compared to measures 17–20?

7. Compare this song with that by Schubert (Ex. G). Examine the phrase structure, modulatory scheme, melodic style, function of the piano, use of chromatic harmony, texture, etc.

8. How does Wolf conceal the similarity of the cadences in measures 7-8 and 15-16? How does he weaken the possible cadential effect in measure 12, and by what means does he strengthen the cadence at measure 16?

9. What is the function of the D♯ in measures 14 and 18? Why does it not cause a modulation?

10. What nonharmonic tones are used? Where are there six-four chords, and how are they resolved?

Table of References

Apel, Willi, *Harvard Dictionary of Music,* Harvard University Press, Cambridge (Mass.), 1944.

Blom, Eric (ed.), *Grove's Dictionary of Music and Musicians,* 5th ed., St. Martin's Press, New York, 1955.

Kirkpatrick, Ralph, *Domenico Scarlatti,* Princeton University Press, Princeton (N.J.), 1953.

Mitchell, William, *Elementary Harmony,* 2nd ed., Prentice-Hall, New York, 1948.

Piston, Walter, *Harmony,* W. W. Norton and Co., New York, 1941; rev. ed., 1948.

Sessions, Roger, *Harmonic Practice,* Harcourt, Brace and Co., New York, 1951.

Index *